PURSUING
SEXUAL
WHOLENESS

PURSUING

SEXUAL

WHOLENESS

ANDREW COMISKEY

Charisma®
HOUSE
Books about Spirit-Led Living

PURSUING SEXUAL WHOLENESS by Andrew Comiskey
Published by Charisma House
A part of Strang Communications Company
600 Rinehart Road
Lake Mary, FL 32746
www.charismahouse.com

Unless otherwise noted, all Scripture quotations are
from the Holy Bible, New International Version.
Copyright © 1973, 1978, 1984, International Bible
Society. Used by permission.

Library of Congress Catalog Card Number: 89-80824
International Standard Book Number: 0-88419-259-8

01 02 03 04   16 15 14 13
Printed in the United States of America

Dedication

This book is dedicated to my wife, Annette,
whose loveliness is immeasurable.

Acknowledgments

Thanks to Kenn Gulliksen for initially entrusting the ministry of Desert Stream to me; to Jim Kermath, who continues faithfully to pastor me and make sure that Desert Stream has a home in the Vineyard Christian Fellowship of Santa Monica; to Leanne Payne, who pioneered the ministry of healing for the sexual sinner; to Klara Steinemann for typing the book as it slowly emerged; to Jody Spinuzza for directing Desert Stream while I wrote the book; and to the men and women of Desert Stream Ministries, whose courage in embracing the fullness of Jesus has rendered them true disciples.

Contents

Foreword

In many years of praying for and seeing the healing of men and women who suffer with gender inferiority and confusion, I've been rendered almost incredulous at times to see how quickly these people can mature into strong Christians—even creative leaders in the body of Christ. Andy Comiskey is a prime example. Barely more than thirty, busy with education, marriage and a family that has quickly blossomed into three sons and a daughter, Andy has not only managed to grasp the key principles of the healing of persons, but he has also put them into an extraordinarily fine system of teachings that will benefit the church worldwide. All this he has done while, as he relates in these pages, he was and still is being healed himself.

Why do some come out of the deepest clutches of homosexual sin and neurosis and then exhibit a growth in Christian maturity and a humble respect for truth and reality that's hard to find in the church today? Is the plight of homosexual sufferers so critical that the Lord accelerates His work of healing and maturing in their souls? No, I've discovered this is not the case.

The fact is that the one who has dealt successfully with

the homosexual neurosis has had to recover truths within our Christian faith and within the makeup of our souls that are, for the most part, obscured or missing today. These are the very things Andy deals with in this book. For example, he writes extraordinarily well about gender wholeness, and this in a day when few believe in the reality of gender, much less that it is rooted in God Himself and that it's a vital aspect of the image of God in each of us. But this is a necessary truth. A man, to be whole, must find affirmation of his true masculinity; a woman, affirmation of her true femininity.

The irony of this is that few *heterosexuals* emerge from adolescence having secured this affirmation of themselves as persons. Although it's seldom understood or dealt with as such, most of the need for therapy and counseling today is directly related to an imbalance of some sort in one's masculine or feminine identity. The need for the heterosexual, though much the same, is simply not so evident as the need Andy expressed.

When people suffering severe gender confusion find healing, it's evident to everyone. Such people are either being made whole or they aren't. Others can cover up their lack of wholeness a little better. They can continue to favor the little heresies of the day that allow them to live more or less self-centered lives and excuse conscious sin. But not the Andys. Christianity either works for them or it doesn't, and they cannot opt for a pseudo-Christian faith. The Andrew Comiskeys mature quickly into giving persons because they have opted for the real thing. They become leaders because they're receiving the powerful, healing word God is always speaking. In this communication they rediscover prime principles about their own souls and the souls of others. This is the value of Andy's book.

Only the authentic gospel will do for sufferers with

homosexual problems. Their need (really much like that of other emotionally wounded sufferers) is made critical today by the fact that they live in a time when many voices within the church are proclaiming other ''gospels,'' other ways of being ''saved.'' These voices invariably center on man's needs and have nothing to say about a holy God, one whose very holiness, when we come into His presence, starts the process of healing and redemption in our souls. Instead of being taught to look up and worship, we're focused on our problem.

For homosexual (like any other) sufferers, failure to learn better is fatal. It is only by focusing on a holy God that they will ever understand their need, much less be able to receive help for it. They are overtaken with that which is decidedly unholy, and they cannot rise out of it short of being ushered into the presence of a God who would rightly father and affirm them.

This is a hallowed fathering. Not everyone wants it. Not everyone chooses redemption. Not everyone accepts heaven and the incredible pain and joy of *becoming in God*. But we need at least to know our options. Homosexual sufferers who make a decision concerning sin and elect to be hallowed (made righteous) in God necessarily come to terms with the *holiness* of God. Not that they can ever understand it: it's too high, too other, yet available to the most depraved souls who confess their unholiness.

We live in an age that reconciles good and evil, and the very language of our day, the coin of our communication, is man-centered. It is therefore filled with psycho-babble. This is what makes the plight of homosexuals so treacherous. They live in a time when even the church has received into itself a false light, a false compassion that is as cruel as death. And rather than being empowered by a holy God to call the sinner to repentance and then heal the needy soul, the church at large babbles on in the language of a lost society. Much to my joy, however, the gospel Andy Comiskey preaches is the authentic good news.

—Leanne Payne

Introduction

Can a homosexual change? The question is much simpler than the answer. I'm not referring merely to stopping certain behaviors or refusing a label. I mean, can a person with predominantly homosexual feelings ever hope to nurture appetites and relationships that are distinctly heterosexual?

I raise the question because I hope to give a clear, multifaceted response to it in this book. Homosexual strugglers *can* change. But they cannot accomplish the transition alone. A purely self-motivated effort will fail because of the deep and powerful roots of sexual identity. Change occurs only, however slowly, as they submit the struggle to their Creator and Redeemer, as well as to trusted others who stand with them in the process of becoming whole.

That process is my own. I stand in awe of my heavenly Father's capacity to effect change and to uphold me in His love along the way. This journey from a homosexual to a heterosexual identity has been revelatory. It has shown God's heart toward me: a compassion faithful enough to abide with me, even in darkness, and powerful enough to expose the darkness and awaken the weak, unaffirmed areas within. I would like to share part of that journey with you in the chapters that follow. I do so in the hope that fellow strugglers—those who seek freedom in any besetting area of difficulty—will be encouraged to trust the Lord where He is needed most.

Before proceeding with my story and truths I've learned as I've struggled and grown, I want to offer a couple of thoughts. First, mine is not a "gay rags to straight riches" account. I'm not villainizing homosexuals and glorifying heterosexuals. The latter can be more messed up than the former, only oblivious to the mess because of the supposed normalcy of their orientation. Rather my story describes a spiritual realignment that had profound implications for how I saw myself in relation to others.

In union with my Creator, I was challenged and enabled to grow up relationally. That involved growing out of homosexuality and into *whole* heterosexual expression. But my sexual transition was more of a natural outworking of the process of growing up, *not its expressed, primary goal*. Accordingly, one must understand sexual reorientation in the greater context of *maturation*, a process that involves one's emotions, intellect and spirit and the utter need for all three to be informed and renewed by the Creator.

Second, I hope to round out the rather flat, inhuman portrayals of spiritual transformation that we often witness at church or in religious broadcast programming. We have become acclimated to the sensational but close-ended testimony: "I was lost. Enter God. Now I am this. The end." It gives us a certain security to think that the murderer will never murder again, the drug addict will stay forever clean, the adulterer will remain pure in his marital devotion, and the homosexual will never have a homosexual thought again.

Welcome to reality. Problems related to sexuality are

deep-seated and powerful. They take time to be resolved. And that process of change is dynamic, subject to fits and starts—inspired victories and unexpected struggles. My course of healing is no exception. I can say God has wonderfully freed me to love as He wills, but He isn't finished, nor am I. Troublesome, immature tendencies remain in me that require His grace and power and the patience of my intimates.

Lastly, don't misconstrue my story as the quintessential homosexual success story. My experience is unique, as is every person's. Although common variables exist that undergird the homosexual struggle and its resolve, these variables take a different form for each. Similarities or differences aside, may this account inspire you to trust more fully in the Creator of your humanity, who is also the Redeemer of its brokenness.

In addition to this book, I have prepared a companion guidebook also entitled *Pursuing Sexual Wholeness*. Each can be used alone, but they are best when used together. At strategic points in this book, I refer to related reading in the guidebook, and the assignments in the guidebook include readings in this book.

ONE

My Story

Childhood has become a series of fond memories for me due to the support and stability of my family. There were no obvious abuses in parenting, no pointed traumas that broke my sense of self. I was clearly loved. Chicken pox and changing instruments in the school orchestra were about the extent of crisis that arose in our nicely suburban context. All was apparently well. These were no red-flag contributing factors to my homosexuality.

Both of my parents were committed to humanistic values. Each stressed the positive in people, downplayed personal evil to the point of denying it (especially my father), and actively engaged in bettering our society. My dad taught psychology at a local college. Over the course of a decade, my mom pursued her education and landed a job teaching child development at the same college. Neither was ignorant in the principles of parenting. Their religious views were initially expressed in Unitarianism. Around the time of my birth, however, Mom switched over to the Episcopal church, where my two older brothers and younger sister (all spaced two years apart) were baptized and later confirmed.

In my parents' families of origin, both experienced a kind of emotional detachment that at times bordered on no connection at all. My mother was orphaned at birth, then adopted two years later. Mom was a model child and faithful to her parents until their deaths. Still, she never seemed particularly bonded to them. Their relationship appeared somewhat forced and formal, as if Mom was obligated to distant relations, not immediate family. Some inner resolve compelled her to become the dynamic woman she was and is.

My father's parents divorced around the time of his birth, leaving him, his older brother and younger sister to grow up quickly. His mother worked long hours in retail, and his older brother died when Dad was about twelve. At fifteen, he had a visit with his father, who while drunk made contact with a prostitute in the presence of his son. His father later died of alcoholism in a veterans' hospital. Dad's mother was a good-hearted but rather unstable woman who was never sure of the affection of her son and daughter. In terms of emotional reserve and a strong commitment to autonomy, Mom and Dad were well matched.

I describe the early, unconscious development of my homosexual tendencies at the beginning of chapter seven. At this point it's enough to say that I became aware of distinctly homosexual feelings at about twelve years old, a

18

fittingly bleak realization for the dark years ahead. Acceptance by my peers was everything to me. Family ties were weak, and thus I wholeheartedly sought to establish a niche with my peers. Most of my time and energy were squandered on striving for acceptance with an ''in group'' of young men who dropped me when it was rumored I was a homosexual. My awful secret became a social crime that resulted in a year's worth of pointed accusations. So much for peer acceptance.

I managed to get by with the help of some strong female friendships that were secure, although ultimately limiting. Within this strange buddy system, I was a neutered ''friend,'' providing the girls with a safe and sensitive companion who proved to be no romantic threat.

I remember feeling constrained by my social-sexual dilemma, aware of growing too old to see women as playmates and yet not growing out of the paradox of fearing men while increasingly hungry for erotic and emotional fusion with them. I coped with the situation by getting involved with a woman for about six months.

In spite of physical involvement and some genuine bonding with her, my homosexual appetite deepened. And at sixteen years old, while my girlfriend vacationed with her family, I had my first homosexual relationship with an old junior high school buddy who four years earlier had rivaled me as the target of homosexual jokes. Together we realized in action what we had been accused of for most of our teenage lives. I thought I had found my one-and-only friend-lover-completion in this kid; my girlfriend was dropped in turn. Several months later, however, our union rather painlessly dissolved after I realized mutual masturbation can't overpower mutual immaturity. The former prevailed, and I set out to discover the bigger homosexual picture of which I had gotten a taste.

I did so with an old female friend; together we began to frequent gay discos in Los Angeles. Soon a group of us became regulars at certain seductive hot spots in Hollywood. I found a niche, a unique sense of purpose and identity far removed from the mundane realities of my suburban roots. My struggle temporarily ceased. I was finally free to align my identity and relationships with my feelings.

Together, my gay friends and I discovered a refuge from the straight majority, whom we concluded were the major barriers in our struggle simply to be ourselves. In fact, we felt slightly superior to those still bound by the cultural conservativism that judged heterosexuality more righteous than homosexuality. The gay self, within the sensual, intoxicating walls of the bar or disco, knew no limits. My youthful body and idealism gave me bargaining power. I loved being wanted and exchanged my marketable qualities with those who seemed to embody mature masculine attributes.

But sexual fusion with an image of masculinity was a far cry from actually possessing that image and making it my own. In fact, attempts at postorgasmic friendship were short-lived. At night we were like little boys working hard to fit into men's bodies, struggling to prop up an image of masculine appeal in order to attract the lost father of our youth. But morning after morning revealed the impoverished capacity we shared to view one another beyond our childish need.

After high school my friend and I moved into a predominantly gay part of town. Obviously, this quickened my involvement in homosexuality. So did my university studies in psychology and sociology, which reinforced the rightness of embracing my homosexual orientation. A large, well-organized gay students' union at the university further secured my homosexual status as normal and acceptable.

Still I questioned it. Many times I found myself staring at the activity before me at a gay bar or party, wondering what I was doing there. So much craziness! Under the banner of the raised phallus, professional, middle-aged men were rendered despondent, even violent, by flirtatious teenagers. Even the most earnest encounters too quickly digressed into erotic play. A good friend was found decapitated after accepting a ride from a murderer preying on young, gay men.

I watched my roommate grow increasingly erratic, from intense highs to more-intense lows, as he struggled through a series of painful "love" relationships. He was unusually handsome and he had the natural capacity to get what he wanted. I recognized in his despondency a bit of my own. I began to ask myself seriously, Do I want to be in this position twenty years from now, hitting and missing in this strong pull to be loved by men?

I was starting to dislike myself as well. Recognizing the futility of quick sex and the self-absorption that accompanies it didn't free me from either. I could observe the desperate and deceitful elements of the gay life, but I still participated in it actively.

Fortunately, some hard realities caught up with me at this point. I had several bouts with venereal disease and anal warts, one of the latter resulting from a group rape. (I had gone home with one man and was assaulted by a dozen.) I also threw myself into a supposedly monogamous relationship that revealed more clearly than ever that neither I nor he nor any other partner could satisfy the deep craving I had to love and be loved.

Wooed by Jesus

I wasn't consciously aware of Jesus' wooing me in this painful season. I did know of Him, though. His transforming power was evident in my two older brothers, who in their late teens had embraced Christian faith with all the fervor and countercultural trappings that characterized the "Jesus people" movement spearheaded by Chuck Smith in the early 1970s. They set a spiritual precedent for me. Their witness said that becoming a Christian meant change, a fundamental reorienting of allegiances toward Jesus that in turn rendered you a different person. Yielding that kind of control scared me to death.

My brothers prayed for me and witnessed to me; I resisted with trite, humanistic apologetics and ridicule. Their prayers won out.

Two significant interactions happened here. My paternal grandmother was a strong believer; in fact, her faith ignited my oldest brother's, eliciting a kind of chain reaction of conversions throughout our family. But she became senile at the end of her life and lived in a convalescent home. I visited her at the zenith of my decadence and doled out some thin condolences. She saw right through me. Surprisingly lucid, she stared at me and said, "You're a phony." She was right. Even sincere efforts at love were overshadowed by the darkness permeating my life.

A connected incident involved my mother. I visited my parents' home one day looking haggard. Mom simply encouraged me to look into the Jesus who had wrought so many good changes in my brothers. That confirmed what the Holy Spirit was gently revealing to me: I needed a new start, and Jesus was the springboard.

While still living with my gay best friend and still in the throes of a supposedly committed gay relationship elsewhere, I accepted Jesus as Lord. Some friends from high school invited me to a Christian concert. When at its end the lead singer gave an altar call, I didn't hesitate a bit. My time had come—God had made the way for me to embrace Him through His Son. My heart grasped what my head didn't yet understand. I became a Christian that night, and the Holy Spirit began to establish Himself as the guiding force in my life.

I don't want to downplay the impact of that decision to follow Jesus. Nor do I want to play it up as *the* threshold over which I blissfully crossed into full heterosexual response. Rather my acceptance of Jesus was the first step of many in the process of becoming whole. He became the basis of wholeness upon my conversion; relationship with Him mediated that wholeness. As with any new relationship, this one was raw. I'm grateful His faithfulness prevailed.

I had little difficulty giving up my current lover. The roots were shallow, and the prayerful support of my downstairs neighbor (a Christian, I discovered) enabled me to break off the relationship. Far more challenging was the reality of living in the gay community while trying to nurture newfound Christian conviction. In other words, my love for Jesus was not matched by a loving community of fellow believers. I felt alone in my faith. I drove into Christian fellowship and drove home to the gay community, where roommate and friends tended to write off my conversion as another amusing tangent.

My personal walk with Jesus, plus the support of a couple of Christian friends who knew of my sexual struggle, enabled me slowly to become rooted in the Christian community. What a transition! The gay community had given me an identity and a support system. Over and against the straight scene and its often harsh and ignorant response to homosexuals, the gay community had provided a haven within which my inner conflict was eased, my homosexuality reinforced. I learned that the church attempts to do much the same thing for those seeking Jesus! In the meantime, I had a lot of divesting and reinvesting to do. The pain of loss ensued. No guarantee of emotional fulfillment existed.

I recall walking into one of the several "mega-churches" in Orange County where young Christians like me congregated to hear concerts and evangelical appeals. Literally thousands of us had gathered, yet I felt alone. I struggled not to discount as irrelevant the blond-haired, blue-eyed enthusiasm that surrounded me. Even a small Bible study group led by my brother failed to provide an effective bridge into the mainline heterosexual church. In my pride and alienation I would resort back to the gay community, looking up an old friend for sexual relations or at least losing myself in a drug-induced high. I rarely questioned the presence of Jesus in my life, but I ricocheted back and forth between the then-limited returns of Christian fellowship and the safe and familiar releases found within the gay community.

Strangely enough, the sin question involving homosexuality was settled very early. The Holy Spirit had opened my eyes to the personal and corporate brokenness of homosexuality while I was still earnestly pursuing gay lovers. It thus came as a confirmation to hear a traditional teaching on a biblical view of homosexuality. I already knew that my sexual identity needed to be redeemed! To hear Paul describe homosexuality as a kind of idolatry (see Rom. 1:16-32) or as one of many sins for which Jesus had atoned (see 1 Cor. 6:9-11) made sense to me. I had no difficulty grasping the fact that I was a sinner who was utterly dependent on the grace of Jesus.

Growing Slowly

Gratefully, in time, I became open and accountable to a small group of Christians with whom I came *to live out* the truth that I was a sinner like everyone else. It wasn't enough for me not to stigmatize myself; I needed to be known and upheld by fellow Christians. One male friend's battle with heterosexual pornography, a woman's loneliness in the long absence of male suitors, another friend's need to give up a heterosexual relationship due to its immature, promiscuous nature—all three experiences resonated with mine and caused us to support each other meaningfully without my or anyone else's being tagged *the* pervert. Rather we were united in our desire to start over with Jesus at the fore. We wanted Him; we needed each other. The great new thing He wanted to do in our lives overshadowed whatever our broken starting points were.

That love from my brothers and sisters made real the hope of coming out of homosexuality and into the fullness of His will. Although the specifics of that will were yet unclear, I knew He could be trusted. I pledged my allegiance to Him.

My pledge was tested in two major ways. The first involved the reality that a growing number of Christians were embracing homosexuality as God's will for their lives. At the university I attended, I stumbled on a study group entitled "The Bible and Homosexuality." There I met pro-gay representatives from almost every Christian denomination. I heard dramatic testimonies from several who professed a kind of "born again" experience upon coming out of their Christian closets and into homosexuality. I met a wonderful woman from the gay church (the Metropolitan Community Church) who introduced me to a handful of earnest gay Christians. I even attended a couple of services at her church. Their testimonies moved me—the wilderness experiences of seeking Jesus in powerless and ignorant religious climates, wanting deliverance but finding none, then leaping to the conclusion that Jesus must want to bless their homosexuality.

Not only did their experiences move me, but they also

tempted me. How great! I thought. The blessings of faith combined with the strong arms of a male lover. The prospect had a powerful appeal, for although Christian life was improving, I still longed for tangible, masculine love. But something struck me in their stories that seemed inherently alien to the gospel. Little, if any, glory was given to the transforming power of Jesus. I drew on my limited knowledge of Jesus and how He called people to Himself; He demanded they submit to Him all that they were, so that He might reorient their personhood and purpose.

In contrast, these pro-gay Christians were expressing more of the glory of their gayness than the honor of Jesus. Their homosexuality was no longer submitted to His scrutiny but held fast as a kind of personal right. In short, I intuited a profound lack of inspiration in their faith. However wounded by the church and sincere in trying to heal the pain, these pilgrims were not anointed.

I left that group, as yet unsure of how God would resolve my sexual struggle. But I was still confident He would resolve it. I wasn't always a faithful yielder of my homosexual yearnings, however. As these last few paragraphs suggest, my early Christian walk was quite unsteady. I grew in faith and fellowship, then would be overtaken by need and loneliness and seek to cover myself in homosexual sin. My old roommate tired of my erraticism. He exhorted me from his pagan vantage point more plainly than most Christians: "Make up your mind. If you want to be a Christian, do it. If you want to be gay, do that. Just quit using me as you swing from decision back to indecision." I, too, grew weary of going strong for Jesus for a season, then opting for the homosexual escape clause when the going got rough. Something had to give.

Here lay the second test of my allegiance to Jesus. Would

I, if given the opportunity for homosexual intimacy, still opt for Him? One-night stands were one thing, but what about the consistent care of one man? I had to admit that at some corner of my heart I was holding out for "Mr. Right." That corner had to be faced and forsaken if I were to forge ahead wholeheartedly with the Lord.

I met Michael during one of my escape routes into the gay scene. He was sensitive and strong, primed for a relationship. We became lovers, and over the next four months I faced a crisis in faith of unsurpassed intensity. I wanted him; I wanted Jesus. Our interludes—hidden, drug-induced, illusory with pleasure and promises to one another—clashed with the heaviness and alienation I experienced in the Christian community because of my unexpressed sin. I kept Michael hidden from the light, and as a result I could barely enter into any form of real worship.

One night we were at a gay party together, and the tension reached a peak. I felt like rising out of the constraints of my homosexual party "mode" and proclaiming my true identity as a Christian to everyone there. But I couldn't. I was manacled by my disobedience. I raced out of the house and sprinted down the street, around corners, through parking lots. I didn't know where I was going; I just knew I had to get out of there. I spied a small group of people gathered outside a doorway, and as I came face to face with them, I realized these were my fellow church members who, unbeknownst to me, were congregating there. I was never so glad to have found fellowship.

In a few minutes I went from giddy alienation to the joy of a homecoming. In retrospect these words of Dietrich Bonhoeffer were realized in that moment:

> The prisoner, the sick person, the Christian in exile sees in the companionship of a fellow Christian a

physical sign of the gracious presence of the triune God. Visitor and visited in loneliness recognize in each other the Christ who is present in the body; they receive and meet each other as one meets the Lord.[1]

After that, I knew I had to give up my relationship with Michael. I did, and a ton of bricks lifted off my shoulders. The Lord purged my heart of the illusion of homosexual romance and called me to strict obedience. In one of the few times I've heard from Him audibly, He asked me if I were truly willing to forsake old ways of loving and being loved. Would I trust and seek Him only in the face of being lonely and tempted by homosexual pursuits?

I committed my sexuality to Him at that point—a full two years after having become a Christian. I took up His call to battle. I vowed no longer to allow my energies to be spilled out in sexual excess and illusion. I truly wanted to be mobilized only by His sure word.

Something broke in me. In retrospect, it may have been deliverance from some kind of tormenting spirit. I wholeheartedly yielded my sexuality to the Lord with the undergirding conviction that homosexual pursuits were no longer an option.

Yet sexual struggles still didn't cease. At times I felt overwhelmed by the uncertainty of my relational future. I couldn't have a male lover, much as I sometimes hungered for one. And as yet I didn't have a great desire for a woman, let alone a vision for wife and family. I continued to define myself as alive to God, alive to some good friendships, alive to some kind of higher calling, but still single and celibate without a passionate future in sight.

One afternoon, things got particularly intense. I wrestled with homosexual lust and relented to masturbation. Afterward

I felt awful and cried out to the Lord. Inside I longed for communion with somebody, anybody—I was weary of well-doing *alone*. And I was even wearier of easing my aloneness through the unsatisfying and unreal realm of solo orgasm.

The Lord stilled my heart. He sent His love in waves. It wasn't flesh and blood, but His Spirit deepened in me that day and sustained me. He called me to a more profound level of trust for all my needs, including that legitimate craving for physical and emotional bonding with another. I became acutely aware of His intention to meet me somehow in my sexual confusion and bring clarity and provision.

That provision took shape when I began to yearn for relationship with a woman. The Christian house I lived in confined me to same-sex relationships, and I grew tired of constantly engaging with the masculine. I wanted to explore the ''other,'' woman, out of a newly secured sense of my maleness. I noticed a difference in my approach to the opposite sex this time. Instead of viewing them as mere friends who afforded me more acceptance than men, I began to experience the peril and pleasure of heterosexual tension. That meant entering into the risky business of extending myself to a desired woman with no guarantee of her response. Like men, women assumed the power either to bless or reject me.

Annette

A couple of small-time relationships came and went, but it wasn't until I met Annette that a union of substance began to be established. We met as co-workers in a bookstore, became friends, and developed a warm, trusting relationship that birthed romantic feelings in both of us. She wasn't what I expected, nor was I her imagined lover. I saw her as worldly and tough; she assessed me as a bit too pious for my own or anyone else's good. Both of us were strong and outspoken. This made for a lot of conflict, as well as for a rich and deep passion.

Two themes undergirded our relationship. The first was honesty. Before we even began dating, I told her of my sexual struggle. Nothing related to my sexuality was hidden, which liberated me to be honest about residual struggle and freed her to face her own fears about my status and choose accordingly. In turn I called her on various areas of hurt and deception in her own life. She began to own these and allow me to help her with them.

But before we became engaged, Annette and I needed to develop a true spiritual mutuality. That was the second great underpinning of our relationship. Annette's Christian background differed from mine in that she considered herself a Christian for most of her life and had not experienced conversion in my charismatic understanding. In spite of dissimilar backgrounds, however, we both conceded our need for more of God's powerful presence and in turn began to attend the Vineyard Christian Fellowship of Santa Monica. The community itself, as well as the utter reliance on God's Spirit, changed our lives. We learned how to pray for one another more accurately and deeply and to trust the Lord. When we came to impasses in our relationship, Annette and I received much support from the church.

An interesting part of our relationship was the unfolding of sexual feelings between Annette and me. At first I had only a mild erotic response toward her. We were friends who then deepened our emotional and spiritual commitment to each other. In spite of glimmers of physical attraction, the catalyst for our relationship in its early stages was not erotic. That surprised me, as my homosexual experiences were fueled by "high octane" lust that burned out to reveal an emotional immaturity incapable of sustaining a long-term relationship.

Annette and I took the reverse path. My erotic feelings for her arose out of a trust and an established emotional and spiritual complementarity. I desired her in a way I had never experienced. Physical attraction was birthed out of our relationship; it wasn't its overblown starting point, charged with illusion and seductive posturing. I'm grateful for God's giving me an opportunity to experience my sexuality anew, as He intends. I'm equally grateful for my wife's grace and patience as the Lord awakened in me the devotion and attraction her beauty deserves.

Annette was learning lessons of her own. When I started the Desert Stream ministry, she initially thought it would be but a small part of my greater pastoral vocation. But after a year into Desert Stream, just prior to our wedding, it became clear that God was multiplying our efforts into a full-time ministry. I had graduated from UCLA and was receiving a part-time salary from the Vineyard. A West Hollywood group I led had developed into a more directive teaching-healing format that became what is now the Living Waters program.

I found my hands full with ministry opportunities, and Annette realized that more than ever she felt confined by homosexual strugglers and the wearisome "gay to straight" testimony people were increasingly demanding of me. She wanted to host "normal" Bible studies and direct the Sunday school. She would have preferred it if her husband left his homosexual past behind and moved forward into heterosexual anonymity. She resented Desert Stream, with specific bitterness toward the gays who were demanding so much of me.

Then one night at our West Hollywood meeting, God changed her heart. While glancing around the room, Annette received God's heart for them. He revealed to her the subtle deception of her judgment toward them—the belief that she was more normal, more righteous, less in need of His grace than they were. The Lord broke her heart with the over-whelming power and mercy He held toward those struggling. He also revealed to her how the various struggles she faced issued out of the same human fallenness and necessitated the same grace that homosexual strugglers required. From that point on, she could accept and even rejoice in God's peculiar calling on our lives.

Other Help

I was extremely grateful for two powerful resources that came alongside Annette and me in those early days. The first was the leaders of Exodus International, an umbrella organi-zation that seeks to equip and unify ex-gay ministries. These men and women—Frank Worthen, Alan Medinger, Mary Lebsock, Bob Davies, Robbi Kenney, Lori Thorkelson—loved and encouraged me and eased the sense of alienation and insignificance I often felt being the lone voice of hope for healing in the Los Angeles area. Exodus's annual train-ing conferences enabled me to draw from a whole pool of ministry resources. I continue to praise God for the stead-fast obedience of Exodus's leadership. Without them our journey would have been more perilous and lonely.

Another great gift God gave us was the ministry of Leanne Payne. I read her ground-breaking book *The Broken Image* when it was first published in 1981. The book conveys her capacity to minister the healing presence of God into the wounds, deprivations and deception of sexual brokenness. I was awed by it. It gave me a vision of greater wholeness for myself and for those to whom I ministered. Later I heard Leanne speak at an Exodus conference and received a power-ful healing related to my masculinity. Since then Leanne's ministry has been the key instrument God has used to keep me alive to the greater works of healing He wants to do in my life and in the ministry of Desert Stream.

Even with that help, however, my struggles continued. While I was still in seminary, individual therapy helped me solidify my masculine identity and identify more meaningfully with the men in my life. It also freed me to be more vulnerable and less controlling in my relationships. That had a great effect on my relationship with Annette. She had given so much in terms of her love, support and flexibility to me. She had to be unusually strong to withstand my background and all the unusual demands of ministry and seminary.

But for her to receive my strength amidst all the other priorities in our lives, I needed to demonstrate my willingness to place her first. That was especially relevant after she became aware of having been violently sexually abused as a five-year-old. She needed the freedom to become small, to be protected by the Lord and her husband.

Our covenant group, a small group of close friends who have met for the last five years to pray and forbear one another, was invaluable. Not only did they pray for Annette, but they also supplied the funds we needed for some short-term marriage counseling. That helped us make a successful adjustment to a more whole and balanced way of caring for one another.

We needed to be a strong team, because our family was expanding. While I was still in seminary, Annette and I had three children—Gregory, Nicholas and Katherine. At the time of this writing, we've discovered that Annette is pregnant again! (We have since become parents to Samuel Jon Comiskey.) The love of Annette and my children fills me to overflowing. Fatherhood has proved to be an incredible source of healing and renewal. Pressures aside, I delight in being able to pass on to my kids the joy and strength and discipline that God has worked in me.

The issue of homosexuality now seems small, dwarfed by the more awesome work of family building and building up the body of Christ. On the rock of God's grace, my family and I proclaim His powerful capacity to restore the most broken parts of our personhood. Once submitted to Him and His church, He can even use them for His glory. In the chapters that follow, as I tell more of my story and those of others, I'll explain just how all that can happen.

TWO

A Biblical Understanding of Sexuality

Karen was clearly distraught. Tears fell quietly to the floor from downcast eyes that refused to meet mine. She confessed in a monotone voice how once again she had fallen with her ex-lover, a woman. Shame competed with confusion. She finally looked up and said, "How come I can't let go of her? I'm doing OK, then *bam*—I'm swept away by my need for her. All my best Christian intentions go out the window when she calls."

A Christian for ten years and a teacher in her church, Karen had wrestled with lesbian feelings for most of her thirty-three years. Until the last year she had suppressed them. No one knew of her struggle except Susan, an earnest Christian participating in a Bible study Karen led. In time, Susan sought out Karen for help concerning her own lesbian struggle.

''Pastoral care'' quickly digressed into a lesbian relationship, with both Karen and Susan revealing a powerful craving for distinctly feminine love. In turn, they sought to cover one another and ended up in an all-consuming emotional and physical bondage. In spite of efforts to break off the relationship, both women found themselves captivated by the powerful feelings that the other woman had brought to the surface and ignited.

Jim faced a similar dilemma. He, too, had been a Christian for a while, but unlike Karen and Susan, he had been involved in the homosexual life-style. Prior to becoming a believer, he had identified as a homosexual and surrounded himself with other gays. During his four years in that life-style, he had engaged in many short-term sexual relationships and several that lasted three to four months.

Becoming a Christian enabled Jim to begin to get free of his homosexual activity. He saw his own brokenness and that of his companions. But he couldn't shake his craving for masculine love. He stopped most of his homosexual behavior, but even in the church, he experienced his sexuality as still homosexual. He could act differently, but his feelings hadn't changed.

Jim sought my help in a state of shame, as had Karen. He confessed to me a new and baffling battle with pornography and anonymous homosexual activity. ''I hate to admit it,'' he said, ''but one night I got real lonely. After a couple of drinks, I felt no qualms about picking up a gay pornographic magazine. It surprised me how powerful the images were. I realized how much I still wanted a man. Ever since then, I get a magazine or a video about once a week and masturbate. Sometimes I'll meet someone and do it with him. I hate myself for it, but it's like I'm hooked. I know it's a bad scene. But how much worse is it than living with feelings that have no outlet?''

Jim's tone bordered on despair. He needed some real answers to questions concerning the steadfast, powerful nature of his homosexual tendencies. The primary question: Why are these feelings not going away? Both Karen and Jim are committed Christians. Yet given their sexual struggle, they both wonder where Jesus is in relation to their homosexuality.

The Nature of Sexuality

Some insights into the nature of sexuality may be helpful here. First, sexuality involves a lot more than mere behavior. It includes a heartfelt yearning for connection with another. At the core it's not a lustful, seductive exercise; it grows from that God-inspired desire within each of us to break out of the walls of the lone self and merge with another human being. Intercourse is only one expression of this merging, albeit the most obvious.

Sexuality involves longing and desire. The body longs for human touch; the soul desires a companion to ease its aloneness. Such yearning is not a concession to our fallenness. According to the Bible, God deemed Adam—*prior* to the fall—as not suited to being alone (see Gen. 2:18). The Creator shaped a complement for Adam to provide for his unique emotional and physical needs, as well as for hers. (For further definition of sexuality, please see *Pursuing Sexual Wholeness* guidebook, pp. 13-14.)

Although Adam and Eve had clear access to God, He realized they needed something more. So He provided for each the gift of the other. And He graced them with an inspired recognition of the limitations of self and a yearning for something greater in union with the other.

How does this apply to Jim and Karen? Both have a strong yearning to connect with others. Unlike Adam's inspired yearning for Eve, however, Jim and Karen long for someone of the same sex. They can be described as having homosexual tendencies because their sexual feelings are geared toward the same sex rather than the opposite sex. Homosexual *behavior* cannot be a valid criterion for whether or not the *tendencies* exist; obviously, one can have the feelings and not act on them. A person who experiences these feelings from preadolescence into adulthood—feelings that remain strong and maybe even intensify—is dealing with homosexual tendencies.

I hesitate, however, to label Jim, Karen or anyone else as *homosexual*. To do so implies a more fundamental definition of the person's humanity. "I am Jim, and I am a homosexual" strikes me as a far more binding status than "I am Jim, and I am dealing with homosexual tendencies." The latter conveys the reality that Jim is not synonymous with his homosexuality. Gay feelings are part of his personhood but need not be *the*, or even *a*, primary reference point. Defining him as *a homosexual* seems to give those feelings an inordinate power to identify him.

But why shouldn't those feelings define him? They've motivated him most of his life. In Karen's case, she spent a good deal of energy suppressing them. When she could do so no longer, the power of these feelings drove her into a relationship that shook the foundation of her ten years of Christian discipleship. Furthermore, sexuality is a basic and potentially life-giving part of being human. Is it any less human simply because the object of desire is of the same sex?

To answer that question, we must dig deeper than the power of feeling. Intense sexual feeling cannot alone determine what is basically true about one's sexuality and one's humanity

38

in general. For example, a husband who longs ardently for his neighbor's wife should not allow the power of feeling to validate adulterous action. He can admit the longings while not ascribing ultimate authority to what his heart dictates.

Second, the ultimate authority to inform and control the heart's desires belongs to the Creator alone. And how critical is that clear word from God! The confusion and discouragement faced by those who have wrestled with homosexual tendencies for years is enormous. Many pray for release but find none. All they know is that their longing for same-sex love intensifies and motivates them to act in ways that months or years before would have been unacceptable to them. The power of the feelings at hand must be faced. And having faced it, each struggler needs to submit the reality of those impulses to the Creator, to grant Him His rightful place as Lord and Redeemer of the struggle.

That gives Him an opportunity to reveal His heart. God wants the homosexual struggler to enter into the fullness of His love. And out of His love, He wants us to love others in a way that reveals who we really are; He also wants *to enable us* to love others in that way.

The Genesis account of creation suggests that from the beginning we have been utterly reliant on the grace of the Father to know who we are and how we're to love. After creating everything else, God placed a unique call upon His human creation. We alone are graced by God to bear His likeness (see Gen. 1:27). As bearers of the divine image, we're in a spiritual relationship with the Creator. We're not mere animals left to our own instincts or desires. And we need to know the Author of the image we have been chosen to bear, for without that connection we are unable to become truly alive to the inspired aspects of ourselves. Like orphaned children bearing the likeness of their father, we may be unable to unite with aspects of our inheritance due to separation from the source. The Genesis account makes it clear: we must know God in order to know ourselves.

God also tells us that to discover our true humanity, we must be known by the opposite sex. A fundamental part of our bearing the divine image is its heterosexual reflection. God created man in His image as "male and female" (Gen. 1:26-27). And in Genesis 2, when God determined to create a helper for Adam, no mere animal would do. The only adequate counterpart was one who would be similar enough to him to meet him on the inspired ground of his humanity, but unique enough to draw him out of his aloneness and fill in the empty places of his masculine soul. From Adam's rib God created Eve (see 2:21-23). And He built into each a yearning for the missing part within that the other possessed.

Adam knew his maleness in the gaze of Eve's distinct femaleness, and vice versa. The uniqueness of each was realized in the other's difference. That dynamic sense of dissimilarity and similarity drew them into an adventure of self-discovery. The mind, body, soul and spirit of the one engaged the other's, probing for common ground and discovering it, as well as the differences that rounded out the limitations of each.

Karl Barth provides added insight into why God created this complementarity of the sexes: "If Eve were only like him [Adam], a repetition, a numerical multiplication, his solitariness would not be eliminated, for such a creature would not confront him as another, but he would merely recognize himself in it."[1]

Becoming "one flesh" (2:24) is a powerful symbol of this coming together. In the act of sexual intercourse, the male and female merge bodies, souls and spirits. United they complement one another, as well as create new life. Bearing the

Creator's image means that humanity, too, can create. Thus, becoming one flesh is more than just a symbol of the hetero-sexual image. It more tangibly reveals a primary blessing upon the image—the ability to create life in a way that reflects the Creator's will. That coincides with God's command to mankind in 1:28 to ''be fruitful and multiply.''

Finally, the union of male and female creates a peaceful, life-giving intimacy. Alive to God and to the glorious pro-vision of the other, Adam and Eve ''were both naked, and they felt no shame'' (2:25). Nothing clouded their love for each other. In their state of innocence, their personal whole-ness liberated an almost boundless freedom to explore and discover all the nuances of their complementarity. Since the temptation to idolatry had not yet been conceived, the Creator reigned over the merging of the creature. Man rejoiced in God for his calling as image-bearer, including the mighty provision of the other. God rejoiced over man and the reflec-tion of His image in the union of male and female.

Thus, the Genesis creation account reveals several key themes. First, God *graces* us with His image. We don't attain to the image; it's a gift of God. Second, the molding of the male and female reveals God's image. The complementarity of the two sexes reflects a fullness of being that same-sex union cannot reflect. Within that complementarity, sexual yearning can be blessed. (For more on the image of God, see *Pursuing Sexual Wholeness* guidebook, chapter 3. See also "A Biblical View of Homosexuality," appendix 2 in the guidebook.)

A Source of Hope

What relevance does this have for homosexual strugglers? Those who are Christians have probably heard much of this before, perhaps trivialized in the slogan: ''If God had wanted homosexuals, He would have made Adam and Steve, not

Adam and Eve.'' That cliche, however, reduces God's intent to something harsh and arbitrary, far removed from the daily battle with homosexual feelings and temptations.

In truth, the Genesis creation account gives hope. It sheds light on the significance of sexual feelings and relationships. It affirms the need to take seriously our yearning not to be alone, to find another with whom we can recreate and procreate. It urges us to probe the transcendent, inspired nature of being male and female. It calls us to be reconciled to the opposite sex and in so doing to discover the uniqueness of our own sex. Most important, the Genesis account proclaims that God is extremely concerned about who we are and how we relate to one another. He doesn't stand back, detached and critical, as we attempt to work out our sexuality. Instead He is deeply committed to our sexual wholeness.

But isn't the person with homosexual tendencies more at a loss here than the average person? Heterosexual bliss in Eden seems light years away from the person who may hardly recall even having desires for the opposite sex. But sexual preference alone isn't the issue. Everyone, regardless of sexual appetites, is light years away from the garden. We continue to be heirs to God's image—male and female in heterosexual covenant. God upholds healthy heterosexuality as His intention for us. But our inheritance from Adam and Eve is more acutely experienced in the fall from innocence described in Genesis 3.

The two chose to be gods. And having partaken of the forbidden fruit, they became masters of their own fate. Alone, Adam and Eve attempted to maneuver a course between good and evil. But such control had dire consequences. They lost the clarity of their true personhood and were unable to reflect wholly the Creator's image.

This loss of intimacy with God led to a breakdown in their

intimacy with each other. We read in Genesis 3:7, "Then the eyes of both of them were opened, and they realized they were naked; so they sewed fig leaves together and made coverings for themselves." No longer could they encounter each other as naked and unashamed. Instead a cloak of fear and guilt obscured the divine image that previously had shone brightly in their union.

The male-female relationship fell from innocence. The entry of sin into the human race cast sexuality into disorder. Every one of us in turn is sexually vulnerable to some degree. People with a heterosexual orientation are no less fallen than those with homosexual tendencies. We are heirs together of the revelation of sexual wholeness in Eden before the fall, but we see that image through a glass darkly. We want that image to be ours but must address realistically the damaged lens through which we view our own sexuality and that of others.

What does this mean specifically for homosexual strugglers? They need a humble recognition of brokenness and a vision of Edenic heterosexual wholeness. Karen and Jim were both acutely aware of their brokenness. Striving for wholeness in the arms or image of the same sex had proved to be a futile and confusing quest. The Genesis account helps explain that futility. God never intended for man or woman to seek completion in the same sex. Thus, homosexual pursuit of erotic and emotional bonding violates something basic to our humanity. The Creator, in His inspired Scriptures, has shown that homosexual feelings and behaviors must be identified as resulting from the fall. Homosexuality is one of the many sexual disorders that have become woven into the fabric of sinful humanity.

Clarity From the Creation

The urge to connect with the same sex remains strong for both Karen and Jim. They need the freedom to admit their feelings and receive compassion. Neither can choose not to have homosexual feelings anymore than heterosexuals can deny their impulse for the opposite sex. But unlike heterosexuals, homosexual strugglers must recognize that their feelings can never culminate in a blessed, one-flesh union. The Genesis account underscores the futility of trying to become whole through a member of the same sex.

Karen came to the point where she admitted to me and to the Lord: "I've been trying to fill a void within me through Susan. There's something about her that touches me unlike anyone else ever has. But it's too powerful. She grips me in a way that throws me off in other areas of my life, especially in relationship to God. I guess I'm coming to see that maybe my desire for her stems from my own brokenness. Maybe she can't free me. The closer I get to her, the more I want. I end up more hungry than ever. Maybe it's healing I need, not Susan."

God's creative will still upholds Karen and Jim. He doesn't abandon them because of personal brokenness, but remains committed to helping them find sexual wholeness. He won't belittle them in the weak and confusing aspects of their sexuality. Instead He wants to grant them a greater vision of real sexual freedom—of what they were created to be.

The prospect of physical intimacy with another devoid of shame and hiddenness surprised them; neither had ever experienced that. Most important, both of them—especially Jim—began to get a sense that their respective genders, however distorted, may be better suited for one-flesh union with the opposite sex rather than with the same sex.

Jim received this vital insight after a bout with pornography: "What I'm seeking in those male images is the kind of man I want to be. I want to be strong and potent. Yet the pornography leaves me feeling more weak than ever. I guess what's really going on in me is some kind of struggle to become a man. I'm struggling to break out of this bound, boyish state. I don't need *a* man. I need to become one. I guess that's what the Adam and Eve thing is all about—a whole man desiring a whole woman."

Thus did the Genesis account give both Jim and Karen a vision for whole heterosexuality. It was only a beginning. Neither was overwhelmed with heterosexual feelings. And both of them were left feeling kind of at a loss. Where were they to go from here? Knowing the truth is one thing; walking out of disorder into God's intended order is another. In the next chapter we'll see how that journey begins by taking hold of the advocacy of God.

THREE

Finding the Greater Desire

Jim radiated enthusiasm. I had never seen him so joyful, especially in contrast to our last meeting two months earlier. At that point he had sunk back into despair concerning his homosexual struggle. In spite of my best efforts to help him gain momentum, he had lost hope. With his usual candor, he admitted he didn't want to keep seeing me. I sadly conceded. Much as I wanted to help, I couldn't make him willing to overcome homosexuality.

But in those two months, God broke into Jim's life. He took a few days off from work to clear his heart and mind. He prayed earnestly for the Lord to reveal His will concerning his sexual struggle. Keep in mind that Jim firmly believed

God's Word. In agreement with the last chapter he upheld the rightness of heterosexuality and the brokenness of homosexual tendencies. But his heart was cracking under the weight of these realizations. He felt constrained by the truth, not set free. The reason was simple. Jim knew the truth *about* sexual ethics. But he didn't know the Father and His profound grace on Jim's behalf. He experienced that awful split between knowledge about God's will and knowing His loving presence at the level of the heart. Jim needed a personal encounter with Him.

God met him at his point of need. While praying, Jim received a powerful vision from the Father, as well as a series of words, that awakened his heart to the reality of God's prevailing grace. God granted him hope, revealing Himself as the greater presence that would guide him through the healing process. The Lord appeared as an eagle on whose back Jim could fly. From that perspective they viewed a vast panorama depicting various scenes out of Jim's life, many of which connoted brokenness, that God told Jim they would need to dive down upon and address. But He assured Jim they would work on them together.

The Lord also ministered words of encouragement and consolation that penetrated Jim's old, fallen world of self-condemnation. Jim received his sonship that day as God's beloved child. Once known by Him, believed in by Him and upheld by Him, Jim became united with the greater presence of God. That freed him to want to get free. The struggle with homosexuality ceased to be an overwhelming reality. With the Lord truly at the helm, Jim could soar and begin to address pointedly his real brokenness.

A New Appreciation of God

Jim is like the majority of people to whom we minister

at Desert Stream. When they first come to us, God has ceased to be a life-giving reality to them. Even though the majority are Christians, the bewildering struggle with homosexuality has constrained the essential flow of faith, hope and love with which God seeks to uphold them. That's why we ask each struggler, Where is God in your homosexual struggle? Is He alive and well and standing with you? Or is He not present at all—detached, disinterested, scornful? In other words, we try to determine how the heart of each individual views God. We know that knowledge about God's goodness may be a mere abstraction that never penetrates the heart.

A lot of this depends on one's cultural and religious background. Some people carry around a much heavier burden of guilt surrounding their homosexuality than others. Many grew up with the topic of sexuality shrouded by shame and secretiveness. In many churches, sexuality is defined by rules saying what you're not to do, especially when referring to homosexuality. Homosexual feelings arise and intensify in these young lives, and their only religious cue has been "Homosexuality is unacceptable and unbefitting of Christians." That quickly translates into "Your struggle with homosexuality is unacceptable to God and His church." Thus, where strugglers need God the most, they may have learned that God is hostile and unavailable.

Furthermore, many strugglers' images of God have been distorted by broken relationships with parents and other significant authority figures. The natural father seems especially important here. Men with homosexual tendencies have often experienced rejection by fathers to whom they never measured up; women have frequently had fathers who abused or belittled them. Many strugglers of both sexes simply did not have an emotionally or physically present father to bless and affirm them, especially in their uniqueness

49

as either male or female. And these negative perceptions of fatherly attributes—inaccessible, untrustworthy and malicious— helped shape their perceptions of the heavenly Father. (For more information, see *Pursuing Sexual Wholeness* guidebook, appendix 1: "The Father Heart of God.")

Karen exemplifies this projection of one's natural father onto the heavenly Father. While she was growing up, her father was distant from the home due to long-standing marital conflict. Then he began to have extramarital affairs, which resulted in Karen's mother's divorcing him when Karen was thirteen. All Karen perceived about the breakup was her father's selfish, immature behavior and the abusive effect it had on her mother, who shared her emotional burdens with Karen. Until this time, Karen had longed for her father's affirmation. She vied for it through good behavior in school and in sports, but she rarely received it. With the breakup of the marriage, she hid her heart from him. Weary of trying to make him love her, and hateful of his distinctly masculine abuses toward the family, she shut him off and refused to feel anything at all toward him.

When Karen became a Christian, she accepted the basic Christian truths that granted her access to God. At a heart level, though, she remained closed off to any real inbreaking of the Creator. Her deep-seated fear and hatred of her father prompted her to protect her heart from the Lord. She would not let down and be vulnerable to Him. Instead she replayed the old, unsuccessful strategy she had attempted with her father—earn His approval by doing good works.

This tendency was also fueled by Karen's homosexual feelings. Assuming God's disdain of them, she worked that much harder to appease Him. She could do a lot for Him, but she couldn't be still and receive His care. Sadly but inevitably, her strategy failed. Homosexual temptation overtook her; she had to step down from church leadership; and, as far as her heart could discern, she had failed God.

Her heart deceived her. What Karen had needed all along was to slow down and be freed of her false images of the heavenly Father—to distinguish between Him and her fallen father. She also needed to begin repairing the damage done by her dad. But most important, she needed a fresh vision of the true and the real—a breaking of God's presence into her heart.

A female counselor who worked alongside me prayed for Karen, awaiting God's move upon her. This took time and much patience, but God gradually revealed Himself to her as a gentle and committed friend, especially in painful memories involving her father's absence and abusive behavior. Karen began to trust the Lord there and to discern the difference between His faithfulness and her natural father's lack of it. During one prayer time, she came to understand how profound was her need for her father's affirmation. She wept and found within the arms of her heavenly Father the gracious, steadfast love she had been striving after since childhood.

Our experience at Desert Stream (as well as my own journey) shows that such spiritual renewal needs to occur before strugglers press into the specifics of sexual brokenness. That's why the ministry of Desert Stream Ministries, and specifically our Living Waters program, makes renewal the top priority. Without first establishing trust in the Father, people are usually unable to share the deep groanings of their hearts. No basis of strength and loving presence exists on which to risk taking hold of the hope of something greater than homosexuality.

But when strugglers discover the Father's supportive love, they find new hope. No longer are they alone, knowing where they should be but living a lie. One greater enters in and undergirds them with His grace. He makes Himself known through a word, a picture, a felt sense of His abiding presence. The Creator reveals Himself as One who does more than just determine sexual order; He also comes alongside and grants the one caught in disorder the assurance of greater realities ahead.

Realigning Desire

In our Living Waters groups, the Father's presence is ministered in a variety of ways, and I recommend our approach to ministries everywhere. The first way is worship. Each meeting begins with praising God and opening ourselves to His move of grace upon us. As we worship, He indwells us and consumes us with His love. The homosexual struggle ceases to be our rallying point as He elevates our perception of ourselves and others to the greater reality of God-with-us. He opens our eyes to glory, that experience of heaven on earth where we corporately bask in His light and power. In many strugglers God awakens that deep yearning to know and be known by the Father. He unblocks the wellspring of faith from apathy and unbelief.

As the current of praise and worship courses through each member, the meeting is transformed from a place where homosexual strugglers commiserate to holy ground where the Creator awakens His people to the greater object of desire—Himself.

That realignment of desire is fundamental to the healing process. Perhaps this explains the relative lack of success achieved by traditional psychotherapy in "curing" homosexuals. A person wrestling with a life-dominating network of desires and distorted self-perceptions cannot be healed by mere analysis of the soul. That soul needs to be encountered by its Creator and bathed in His love, according to His original intentions.

Romans 1:18-32 makes a strong case for this. The apostle Paul explained the powerful role of the Creator in maintaining sexual order and described the sexual chaos that results when individuals shift their focus from the Lord to the creature. Mankind possesses a powerful desire for the good—that innate yearning to worship our Maker and praise the One who ordained life (see Rom. 1:19-20). When that yearning is suppressed, it becomes shrouded by lesser desires. Thinking becomes futile; hearts grow dark (see vv. 21-22). We're vulnerable to all kinds of idolatry when our primary desire is not worshipping the Creator.

All of us, Christian or pagan, emerge out of a broken world that fractures our desire for worshipping the Creator and renders us susceptible to lesser appetites. None of us is exempt from the implications of Romans 1. Accordingly, Paul went on to describe homosexual practices as a potent symbol of desire gone awry. He broadened that example to include a slew of evil thoughts and practices that issue out of the rebellious heart (see vv. 23-32).

The homosexual struggler, like everyone else, needs that fundamental realignment with the Creator. The latent desire for worshipping Him needs to be awakened. And as it is, the Father becomes the primary object of desire. Then He can minister His will and loving presence to such lesser desires as homosexual tendencies.

As the examples of Karen and Jim show, however, that awakening of primary desire may take time, as well as the specific prayer and presence of others. Many remain shut down in a worshipful environment. Those who are heavy-laden with guilt and shame, those saddled by broken parental relationships that distort their perception of God, and those simply bound by a Christian background that emphasized learning *about* God rather than *knowing* Him—all these may be unable to enter the lifegiving flow of worship.

Here we need to learn how to pray effectively. We may have to help people identify the hidden blocks that impede worship, as was the case with Karen. We may need to pray for a greater release of the Holy Spirit in their lives as a kind of spiritual "jump starting" of the heart into a new level of responsiveness. Or, as is often the case, we may simply need to uphold them as children of God until they're able to receive the Father's love and worship Him heartily in return.

The Living Waters Model

The Living Waters group format enables all of the above to occur. We leave a lot of time for waiting on the Lord so He can help us identify and surmount the unseen blocks that prevent participants from entering into worship. He may give words of knowledge or wisdom through the group members themselves; the person to whom that word applies then receives specific prayer and ministry. And in the small groups, participants continue to pray for one another's spiritual renewal. Frustrations and victories toward that end are discussed. For some, the mere encouragement of a brother or sister unblocks them from receiving the Father's care. (I will elaborate on this in the next chapter.) Finally, people are given the grace and the time they need to be able to enter into that life-giving flow of worship. Our patience grows out of faith that His presence will become a greater, living reality in their lives.

The Father, through His direct reach into the lives of strugglers and through the prayers of others who mediate that inbreaking, reaffirms His intentions for the sexuality of His children. Hearts open to receive His love and worship Him are primed to receive fresh vision for their sexuality. No matter how fallen they've become, no matter how overwhelmed by homosexual tendencies they are, God upholds them according to His image—mankind as male and female.

This revelation is key to the healing process. As strugglers delve into the hard realities of their homosexual tendencies, they can never lose sight of the greater picture composed of their gracious Father's constantly extending Himself to them. He offers not only His powerful love, but also the powerful image of sexual wholeness.

Once again, the capacity to receive the truth about God's heterosexual intention will differ from person to person. For many, like Karen, it may take the focused attention and prayer of God's people to minister effectively the reality of their true, heterosexual personhood.

Several of us gathered to pray for Karen. She had recently become aware of having been sexually abused by an anonymous figure in her early childhood. Distraught, she agonized for several hours as we gently prayed for her, giving the Holy Spirit opportunity to help her release the shame, anger and hurt that had been pent up for years. After the sobbing eased, we realized how raw and vulnerable Karen was. She immediately wanted the covering of her ex-lover; the broken child within hungered for the maternal care afforded perversely by lesbianism. In turn we prayed for God's covering over her—for His garment of truth, love and divine protection to clothe her nakedness. Almost immediately, God granted us a vision of a distinctly feminine robe—elegant in its tailoring, rich in texture and dazzling in brilliance. That robe was descending upon her. We discerned it as a royal garment befitting a woman honored by God. But although the robe covered her entirely, it didn't yet fit her. Karen had to grow up into the fullness of God's calling her into whole, heterosexual womanhood. In the meantime, He covered and upheld her in that garment.

''In the meantime'' refers to that exhilarating place between God's gracious call and our daily struggle with homosexual tendencies. In the next chapter, we'll explore in detail how the Father makes a way for greater victories, as well as inevitable struggles, along the path to becoming whole.

FOUR

Jesus—God's Agent of Freedom

She had a history of giving herself to men. In times of emotional or financial insecurity she would offer her body in exchange for a cheap shot of love—or at least a few denarii. Everyone in town knew it. Her own shame was magnified and sealed into her by the penetrating scorn of the villagers. Eventually, she grew numb to her sin and brokenness. Self-loathing and even remorse failed to prompt a change of heart. In the glare of public and personal judgment, she was already damned.

He awakened hope in her. She heard Him speak to a large crowd, and He seemed different from the religious men she saw in town. He wasn't concerned about appearance and tradition. In fact, He seemed more intent on revealing religious hypocrisy than belittling sinners like herself. She could tell He saw the heart. And she began to trust Him with hers, even from afar. Somehow she knew He could free her from the mess she had made of things. He could reverse the judgment she and others had made upon herself.

She spotted Him eating dinner with a well-known religious man. The sight of it made her shudder: reclining on the patio together were the embodiments of hope and condemnation. The One she knew could free her conversed with the one who represented the shame and scorn that bound her. But this was her moment. She had never come this close to Him before. If she wanted to be free, she had to act now, even if it meant facing greater scorn.

The desire to be free prevailed. She entered the patio. Upon facing the powerful compassion of Christ's gaze, she wept. Unable to say anything or even sustain eye contact, she fell to her knees and worshipped Him. She anointed His feet with oil, then kissed and wiped them with her hair. She knew this was her deliverer. His presence transformed her status from untouchable to one embraced by God. Shame and the ravages of her sin ceased to inhibit her. His grace burned off all self-consciousness and compelled her to devote herself to Him.

The religious man was astonished. Jesus knew he would be and explained that profound sin and brokenness, when recognized as such and submitted to the source of forgiveness and restoration, prompt an equally profound level of love and devotion. "That's precisely why," said Jesus, "this woman worships Me freely and unabashedly. You, on the other hand, have been blinded by religious tradition and no longer recognize how profoundly you need to be freed by Me. That's why you continue in heady unbelief. You ask Me tricky questions in the hope of discounting Me, so you can remain unchanged. She submits herself to Me, sin and brokenness intact, and is changed forever. She goes in peace, alive to Me, forgiven'' (Luke 7:36-50, my paraphrase).

The Way

Through Jesus, the Father makes a way for *all* sinners who recognize they have fallen short of His intentions. For the homosexual struggler, the gap between whole heterosexuality and the struggles at hand necessitates a bridge. Jesus is that bridge. The prostitute in Luke 7 came to rely on Jesus in light of her awareness that only He could free her from the burden of sin. The homosexual struggler can likewise come to rely on Jesus. The sin and brokenness wrought by homosexuality need not prevent the struggler from seeking Him out; that heart's cry for wholeness is precisely what necessitates Him! The prostitute knew that, and her heart's cry for wholeness compelled her to break through the veil of shame that otherwise could have immobilized her. The divine image in her was cracked and stained. Jesus called forth that image and reclaimed it as His own.

Jesus is God's agent of freedom for the person whose divine image is marred by homosexuality. He created us to reflect Himself, and where Satan and sin have defamed that image, He prepares the way for its repair. He also realizes how utterly helpless we are to restore that image ourselves. He knows our tendency to disobey Him.

As God's Son, Jesus was the perfect reflection of the Creator's image. He loved and obeyed His Father without relenting to sin. Jesus lived out the faithfulness that we cannot and would not. He stood in our place as the obedient One. As God and man, He willed to reflect to us the true image that the Father longs for us to shine forth.

But Jesus did more than merely exemplify human potential

at its best. In accord with His Father's will, He obeyed unto death. He took upon Himself the brokenness that constrains God's image in us; He also bore the sinful disobedience that issues out of that brokenness. He died with the weight of the slow death that sin works in us. And in His resurrection power, Jesus broke through the hell of all that separates us from the Father, from each other and from who we are as His image-bearers. He freed us to live in the Father's love.

Now Jesus mediates the process whereby the Creator's powerful grace penetrates through the layers of darkness that obscure our true humanity. He reclaims the real image, intent on revealing to us, and through us to all, the masterpiece within.

Jesus is so powerful a mediator because He chose to become alive to the struggles of the human soul. The human Son desired intently to obey the Father, yet He was tempted as well to satisfy Himself and veer off the difficult course established by the Father. That struggle was revealed in Satan's temptation of Jesus (see Matt. 4:1-11). Satan attempted to hook Jesus into the very human tendency to establish authority falsely, to seek self-glory rather than the glory of the Father.

Jesus triumphed by standing firm in the Father's will, but not without struggle. In His humanity Jesus faced the temptation to find security and pleasure apart from the Father's will. How else could Satan truly tempt Him unless he had access to something Jesus had the capacity to desire? So Jesus' humanity assures all people, including homosexual strugglers, that He has, indeed, entered into our dilemma. He can truly sympathize with our weakness, for according to the Scriptures:

> We do not have a high priest who is unable to sympathize with our weaknesses, but we have one who

has been tempted in every way, just as we are—yet
was without sin. Let us then approach the throne of
grace with confidence, so that we may receive mercy
and find grace to help us in our time of need (Heb.
4:15-16).

To elaborate on this theme, we must realize that Christ's
empathy with our struggle against sin is deepened by His
never having yielded to it. The battle with temptation ceases
temporarily when one gives in to the object of desire. Jesus,
in His obedience, had no fleshly escape clause. He held fast
to the Father's will to the end. We can assume in turn that He
was tempted nonstop with an intensity that neither the homosexual struggler nor any other person has ever faced. That
makes His compassion and empathy all the stronger as He
upholds us in our struggles with temptation. As the Scriptures state, "Because he himself suffered when he was
tempted, he is able to help those who are being tempted"
(Heb. 2:18).

Jim experienced that powerful compassion *and* resulting
victory in the course of a same-sex friendship. Having spent
a weekend camping with some male friends from church,
Jim was disheartened by homosexual feelings that arose for
one particular friend. He cried out to the Lord, "Jesus,
I seek Your face. I choose to surround myself with godly
men who don't share my weakness. And then this! Even
in the best setting possible, I can't get away from my
struggle."

Jesus spoke to him gently, "I've been tempted in all ways
as you have, including your struggle with improper sexual
feelings. Don't hate yourself. Look to Me. Let My love and
compassion uphold you there. It's because of your vulnerability that I too became vulnerable to sin and death. And it is
in your vulnerability that you will learn to trust Me. Look

to Me, submit your desires to Me, and you'll share in My victory over sin.''

Jim wept. He entered into the advocacy of Jesus at the level where he needed it most. Instead of contributing to his shame and confusion, the presence of Jesus upheld him. Jesus elevated the desire for his friend to the greater and truer yearning for connection with the masculine. And with Jesus as that primary object of masculine connection, Jim could in turn sort through the feelings for his friend without falling prey to old, false ways of securing it. Jim submitted his temptation to the empathy of Jesus. And in His presence, Jim was freed to enter into Jesus' victory.

In His life of obedience to the Father, Jesus makes a way for us to be obedient. He alone is *the* faithful Son. Only Jesus consistently holds fast to the Father's will. And this is precisely the Father's provision for us in *our* disobedience. By relying on Him and His victory over sin, we enter into that victory, as did Jim, and can remain upright in the face of all the various lures to sin. (For more information on the ministry of Jesus, please see *Pursuing Sexual Wholeness* guidebook, chapter 4.)

Overcoming Brokenness

But what about the powerful brokenness we bring into our relationship with Jesus? Breaking through the domination of sin requires more than empathy, or even inspired help in the face of temptation. Jesus took His life of obedience one step further. He obeyed unto death. In accordance with the Father's will, Jesus took upon Himself the weight of every broken, sinful, demonized angle of our humanity—the whole spectrum of the shattered divine image—and died with it. He did this in order that sin's dominating effect would die once and for all.

He did so for two obvious reasons. The first was to rescue us from death. The second related reason was to shatter the grip of sin in a way that enables the broken image in us to be restored to the Creator's intent. He allowed Himself to be broken by our sin, assuming the weight of homosexual bondage. By that I mean He took on Himself the deceitful, unrelenting burden carried by most homosexual strugglers that daily taunts them: "You are gay—your feelings, your fantasies, your inner being are at core homosexual. You will never be anything else. You are confined to overwhelming homosexual impulses that at best you can suppress."

Jesus bore the burden of life-dominating homosexual tendencies for us! He also assumed the broken, sinful way we have expressed those tendencies in homosexual behavior and relationships. And in so doing, He granted us our central point of victory. He broke sin's power over us by allowing it to break Him unto death and then rising from the grave on the third day. The cross and the empty tomb symbolize that victory. Thus, in the face of struggling with homosexual tendencies and sin, we must look to the greater One and His victory.

We simply agree with His obedience unto death; we submit whatever semblance of sin and death we're experiencing to Him. The burden has been assumed by Jesus. Instead of bearing it ourselves, we release it to Him.

As Athanasius, one of the early church fathers, wrote, "That which He has not assumed, He cannot heal." To set us free from homosexuality, Jesus must first assume the sin and brokenness at the core of the struggle. For our part we must recognize and name the broken aspects of our sexuality and allow Him to assume them. But what precisely are we submitting? I've mentioned several things: death, sin, brokenness, disorder, need. Let me now attempt to distinguish between them and also explain their relatedness.

What We Must Submit

Disorder refers to the theological reality of being part of a fallen creation. God's intended order for humanity has been distorted. Even as we seek to become what He has willed, factors outside and inside ourselves may thwart our desire.

For example, the young person who begins to experience homosexual tendencies at age ten may sincerely want to have normal heterosexual feelings. But a number of factors that are unclear to him have emerged to create homosexual tendencies. Disorder is expressed in those tendencies, as they may inhibit him from growing into heterosexual maturity. Therefore, he needs to confess the reality of disorder.

But the presence of homosexual tendencies doesn't necessarily imply willful sin. We can feel dominated by homosexual impulses and not be in the throes of lustful behaviors and relationships. Most common is the aforementioned yearning for distinctly masculine or feminine love. That yearning actually conveys a deep need for uniting with one's own gender. Here we go back to the true nature of sexuality— the inspired longing for communion, for completion, for a point of genuine wholeness through union with another. That need must be taken seriously and treated compassionately if we're to get free from the domination of homosexual impulses.

We must also submit the *brokenness* that has prevented that need from getting met aright. Here we're often dealing with the breakdown of key relationships that have prevented us from freely and fully embracing our gender. When the sin of others causes the legitimate childhood *need* for proper same-sex love to remain unmet, that need may express itself in homosexual impulses.

Disorder, brokenness and need often result from factors over which the individual has little control. In other words, homosexual impulses in and of themselves do not constitute willful sin. But *sin* does enter into our experience when we say, "I have these feelings and needs, and I'm going to deal with them by getting into a homosexual relationship or engaging in homosexual behavior."

In a sense, strugglers who make that choice are assuming control, a lordship over their own sexuality. The need and brokenness at hand cease to be submitted to God or others who could be healing agents. Instead they try to find release through submitting the impulses to a supposed object of desire. Like Adam and Eve after the fall, the strugglers try to cover up in an attempt to ward off the dreadful sense of alienation that results from bypassing the Creator. The fig leaf this time is a lover, a fantasy, a pornographic image that the strugglers bond with in a futile effort to ease their aloneness. That attempt at self-covering, at meeting one's needs according to the creature's wisdom, not the Creator's, constitutes sin and rebellion. (For more information, please see *Pursuing Sexual Wholeness* guidebook, chapter 2.)

Thus, homosexual sin fundamentally arises out of strugglers' lack of faith in the Creator's capacity to meet their needs. That corresponds with Romans 14:23: "Everything that does not come from faith is sin."

This unbelief may be the result of a number of factors, but the primary one I see with Christians is that their long-standing struggle with homosexual tendencies is never submitted to anyone but God. Shame and fear compel them into their prayer closets; the release in prayer alone is found to be inadequate; and eventually they burst out of their "closeted" struggle and engage homosexually, certain God cannot change them.

What has been entirely bypassed is God's healing as mediated through His body, the church, where the many gifts of the Spirit and aptitudes of various personalities can converge to provide the help God has for the strugglers. Submission to Jesus needs to occur not only in personal prayer, but also in prayer, support and counsel as mediated through His body. Without that mediation, strugglers on the verge of sin may be tempted beyond what they're able to withstand.

The tragic result of homosexual sin is greater brokenness, an inflamed need that is never sated. Sexuality becomes shrouded by evil. Outside the light and protection of Jesus and His church, strugglers submit their bodies, souls and spirits again and again to the deception that another man or woman (or at least idealized images) can complete them. Sensual connection culminating in orgasm is discovered; lost are relationships that affirm the true image. The power of the enemy and the flesh converge to trap strugglers into homosexual lust and greater deception. The commitment to God and His truth concerning sexuality becomes skewed.

Now the creature stands over and against the Creator, shaking his fist at what are interpreted as outdated, arbitrary expressions of an ignorant God and His people. In time, deceived strugglers may grow numb to the witness of order and wholeness that cries out of the true image within. Genuine need and brokenness become anesthetized by sin. Like Paul's description of pagans, strugglers may become calloused to the pain that initially gave rise to homosexual tendencies and may also cease to feel the greater brokenness being wrought by sin (see Eph. 4:17-19).

The ultimate end of sin is death. For the homosexual struggler, this means first an end to his line because of the lack of children. And without Jesus, the struggler's death sentence in this lifetime will continue throughout eternity.

Jesus extends Himself to each struggler, at once poignantly human and powerfully divine. He submits Himself as the bearer of all disorder, and in particular of the brokenness that gives rise to homosexual impulses. He invites the needy one who craves same-sex bonding to submit the yearning to Him out of the realization that He doesn't blame the struggler for possessing the tendency. And He assumes the weight of every sinful effort the struggler has made to resolve that tendency according to his own will and wisdom.

Confession to Jesus, then, involves a lot more than admitting wrongdoing. It's an admission of one's utter reliance on Jesus for every aspect of the struggle: the disorder and brokenness that require His healing, the deep needs that require His guidance, the sin that requires His cleansing and release. If left on our shoulders, that burden would kill us. But Jesus assumes the weight of homosexuality in order to free the struggler to rely on Him fully for its resolve. And as we'll see in Karen's example, that reliance on Christ's suffering is more often than not mediated by other Christians.

How Jesus Reached Out to Karen

As mentioned earlier, Karen fell into a lesbian relationship as a Christian. She had battled alone with the tendencies for a long time, working out her salvation through *doing* Christian activities. Her moral failure hit her deeply. For the first time, she had to confess to Jesus and others the real sin and brokenness in her life. She had prayed about the struggle before. Yet God's response seemed vague and abstract. And up until that point, she had been successful in suppressing her urges.

Now she had fallen, and she faced the risk of submitting some of the deepest and most intense aspects of her life to Jesus, through His body. She faced His presence in the presence of caring brothers and sisters. As Bonhoeffer wrote:

> A man who confesses his sins in the presence of a brother knows that he is no longer alone with himself; he experiences the presence of God in the reality of the other person. As long as I am by myself in the confession of my sins, everything remains in the dark, but in the presence of a brother, the sin has to be brought into the light.[1]

The light of Jesus pierced the shadow of Karen's inner struggle. For the first time, she started to be known for her victories *and* defeats, her strengths *and* her weaknesses. Upon confessing her fall to me, she wept for the first time with another human being about her struggle. Jesus met her through our prayers and the acceptance I extended to her. Together we agreed with Jesus' work on the cross that covered her sin. We laid at Christ's feet the shame and fear that surrounded her struggle. We made plans to pray through the brokenness and desires underlying her tendencies. And Jesus was faithful to minister His profound advocacy and support toward her in a way she had never experienced. She hadn't yet been able to receive it, because she hadn't yet let Him into her struggle through the prayer and support of His people.

But Karen needed something more. Beyond Jesus' bearing the weight of her sin and granting her His advocacy, she needed His authority to rise out of her broken state. Having agreed with His crucifixion, she needed His resurrection power. And that's her inheritance, as it is for anyone who identifies with Christ. His resurrection affirms His authority to resurrect our fallen selves. The same power that raised Him from the dead raises us from the death sin has wrought in our lives. In Karen's case, she needed His resurrection power to resist the powerful pull of her relationship with Susan. As Paul wrote in Romans 6:5-6: "If we have been united with him in his death, we will certainly also be united with him in his resurrection. For we know that our old self was crucified with him so that the body of sin might be rendered powerless, that we should no longer be slaves to sin."

Karen wasn't ready at first to pray for the authority to break off her relationship with Susan. (In the next chapter we'll talk more about the pivotal role of willingness in becoming empowered.) She was unsure because Susan had become everything to her, so the loss of her was overwhelming. But God was faithful. He revealed to her the truth about their relationship—how it was inspired by need and brokenness and even emotional manipulation. Karen began to realize that Susan had overtaken God as the primary desire of her heart. She finally came to the point of desiring the Father first. Only the resurrection authority of Jesus made this possible.

We met again to pray. No fireworks went off, and no Pentecostal cartwheels were turned. Karen simply received the steady assurance of Christ's authority in her that enabled her to break off the relationship with Susan. She also needed His power to seek Him and others daily for support in maintaining a healthy distance from her.

Jesus surprised Karen soon after that empowering prayer. One night she was at home alone, feeling her aloneness with a poignancy and depth that she had never experienced until the breakup with Susan. By sheer force of her will, Karen began to worship Him. Her devotion became more heartfelt and crescendoed following a vision the Lord had given her as a bridegroom. He appeared distinctly human and was beckoning to her as a gentle yet insistent lover seeking His bride. He assured her of her beauty and of the careful, protective nature of His love for her. Would she take His hand and accept His proposal of marriage? He swore to honor His commitment.

Karen accepted and for the first time felt drawn out as a woman by a man in a healthy way. Christ freed her to respond to Him with distinctly feminine, heterosexual feelings. Without any hint of eroticism, Karen experienced that longing for the security and strength of a man's arms. As the true image of God in man, Jesus called out her true image as a heterosexual woman. He did so with care and promised to cover her as she sought to exercise that image in the new relationships that awaited her.

Like the prostitute in Luke 7, Karen learned to trust Jesus in light of her sin and disorder, not in spite of it. He revealed Himself as the One who could assume her disorder, brokenness, need and sin. He empowered her to rise out of sin's constraints. He did this in part through His body, through those willing to stand as His agents on behalf of their sister. Jesus truly became her bridge to freedom and the divine lover of her soul as she sought to learn to love according to the Father's will.

FIVE

Yielding to a Higher Allegiance

As I grew in the early years of my Christian walk, each new accomplishment was matched by a new snare. I was ordained as a pastor at the Vineyard; Annette and I moved to Pasadena, where I pursued a master of divinity and counseling credentials at Fuller Theological Seminary; and Desert Stream flourished. Yet in the midst of it all, I became addicted to pornography. I felt compelled almost weekly to seek sidelong glimpses of softcore porn in liquor outlets and general bookstores.

About seven years had passed since any habitual use of the slime. I was as surprised as Annette when I discovered my impotence to resist it once more. It consumed a lot of time, provoked a lot of shame and revealed the deceitful rhythms of my heart. My sex life with Annette had nothing to do with it; that was full and satisfying. But the lure of the unknown, the uncharted hours in which to pleasure myself, and a world of sensual rewards far removed from the pressures of school and ministry—these captivated and bound me to pornography.

This addiction continued erratically for about two years. In that time I witnessed a shameful and deceptive part of myself that I had never seen before. Annette faced it, too. But with her help, the prayers of our covenant group, and specific accountability with one close friend who struggled in the same way, I overcame the compulsion.

God called me to a higher allegiance. Would I yield the pleasure of sin to Him who required and deserved my love and obedience? As I sought to do so, His grace was sufficient. I learned new lessons in how to stand in the power of the indwelling Spirit and in the support of my intimates. I also developed a new compassion for those hooked into various patterns of sin. The Lord showed me that I still wasn't exempt from bondage; I needed to live out His grace like everyone else.

As I learned so painfully, overcoming broken sexuality requires giving allegiance to a greater desire, desire for deepening intimacy with the Father through Jesus Christ. The struggler yields the cries and yearnings of his heart to the Father. He finds that his Creator has made a way for him through Jesus. Where sin and brokenness have resulted in sexual problems, Jesus enters in and assumes the struggle Himself. All the struggler can do is bow down and worship. The creature desires the Creator and now healer of his soul more than he does the lesser objects of illicit sexual desire.

In this way, the struggler enters into the true rhythm of

72

the Christian life. Having received the Father's care and the provision of Jesus, he then faces the awesome blessing and challenge of committing himself to God. Mere feelings of love and devotion aren't enough; they can be surpassed easily by a flood of homosexual impulses. The struggler must count the cost of commitment. He must ask himself, Will I continue to seek Him when I don't feel like it? When I feel more like entering into a gay relationship or some compulsive habit? When the going gets rough and neither God nor His people seem readily available? When God isn't meeting my expectations of how and when healing should occur in my life? Will I seek Him even then?

In His infinite wisdom and protective grace God demands our allegiance. He searches and refines our hearts in order to cause us to seek Him above all else. He calls us to yield our false ways of meeting our needs, to lay down the cold, hard shell of sin and self-sufficiency. Desiring access to the deep heart, He longs to work in us a tenderness and receptivity to His healing work. And He grants us His power—the resurrection authority of Jesus—to enable us to hold fast to Him throughout the painful and uncertain season of healing that lies ahead.

The true rhythm of the Christian life can thus be defined as receiving His profound care, choosing whether we want to commit ourselves to His care above all else, and in turn rising up according to His power. On that basis we are aligned with the Father and are able truly to benefit from every good gift He offers.

The Role of Willingness

Unfortunately, many homosexual strugglers do not become aligned with the Father in a way that proves ultimately healing. They may enter into His care and begin to taste of

Christ's provision for them. But they find the cost of obedience too great, its rewards too intangible. They may desire to be free from homosexuality at some level, but at a more profound level, their hearts remain aligned with homosexual pursuits. The threat of loss is too overwhelming. Yielding control over their desires and inner brokenness may be too much. As a result, their willingness remains weak, repentance is shallow, and their hearts grow divided between the pursuit of God and the immediate returns of homosexual pursuits.

That fundamental willingness to seek first the kingdom rather than illicit pursuits is a key to healing. For strugglers and helpers alike, the degree of willingness must be ascertained. Otherwise, the motivation of those seeking help may remain veiled. They may be wasting their time and the helpers' time also in pursuing sexual resolve when they still want the immediate returns of homosexual pleasures. In spite of everyone else's agenda for them, they may not be ready to get free.

For example, I counseled a young man whose mother and pastor insisted he seek help. He counseled with me for approximately six months, during which time he discussed many significant aspects of his life. He didn't make any progress, however, in stopping homosexual behavior. He wept over his failures, but not for himself. He felt he had failed his mother, his pastor, his church and God. But he remained true to his own heart, which at that time was intent on homosexual pursuits. His sorrow was not evidence of repentance from sin; it was born out of letting down those who wanted him to repent. Until he wanted that repentance for himself, counseling was a waste of everyone's time.

Willingness is not easily recognizable and may take time to discern. One woman with a warm and engaging nature came to me effusive over the prospect of change. Her sincerity overwhelmed me, and I gave her every opportunity to get help. After she refused the third offer for tangible assistance, however, I realized she wasn't ready. She tried to convince me of her readiness, but it just wasn't there yet.

On the other hand, I met one woman at a healing conference who was as rebellious and manipulative as anyone I had ever met. She came to the conference with her lover. The two made quite a scene together until a dramatic breakup occurred midweek. Then the one promised to seek help through Desert Stream, but I didn't give it a second thought. One month later, however, she moved a thousand miles to receive our help. After a difficult but refreshing three-year period, she was healthy enough to marry a solid Christian man. Underneath her original, rebellious exterior, she had a heart intent on getting free.

A key ingredient in willingness involves discerning what the Lord's priorities are in the strugglers' lives at a given point. His time clock for people's healing may be different from ours. For example, most people with homosexual tendencies need first simply to become rooted in Jesus and His community. It would be premature to insist that they immediately face squarely the specifics of sexual brokenness. By the gentle conviction of the Holy Spirit and the establishment of trust within a Christian setting, they're freed to seek specific help for dealing with their homosexuality. I believe we need to give homosexual strugglers the same grace that we would give any Christian facing sexual identity issues. A person with a promiscuous heterosexual background isn't usually required to give immediate account for past and present sexual activity. That needs to occur at some point regardless of one's background. But that willingness to do so is preceded by a sense of security and trust that renders sharing at such a deep level appropriate. Requiring people to confess and give account for sexual difficulties when they aren't known at less-threatening levels can be a jarring and needlessly painful procedure. It may actually block their willingness to be healed, not inspire it.

We've seen this gradual process work in many homosexual strugglers who attend the Vineyard before knowing about Desert Stream. Often they're initially skeptical of the latter. They presume it is some kind of brainwashing club for aging homosexuals. But in time those who become committed to the church recognize the depth of their need for help. And one by one they seek out the various avenues of assistance available to them. What's key here is that God's first priority for each is to get rooted in the greater Christian community. Then, building on that foundation, He reveals the heart's need for a deep level of healing.

Jim was one such individual. He began attending our church soon after his conversion. Still in the midst of the gay community, he wasn't ready at first to address all the brokenness wrought in his life by homosexuality. I discerned his struggle, and in a friendly fashion I introduced myself and the ministry to him. However, I didn't insist that he confess all and commit himself wholeheartedly to Desert Stream. He simply knew it was available to him. I had to resist the temptation to impose upon him my understanding of what he needed to be free. Instead I committed him to prayer and put the burden of readiness of heart on the Lord, understanding that it's His Spirit, not my insistence, that prepares the heart for healing. I had to continue to yield Jim's need to the Lord. So I addressed him merely as a Christian man, not an unresolved homosexual. And in time Jim sought me out for specific help. In prayer one day, beleaguered by homosexual fantasies and loneliness, Jim received a word from the Lord to call me. That was the beginning of his in-depth healing process, which I will continue to detail throughout this book.

Those Who Resist the Word

For Jim and the others mentioned thus far, God was able to work a willingness for greater healing because, at the core, each responded to His convicting Word that defines homosexuality as sin and brokenness. But what about those who resist that Word? The most important thing to bear in mind is that God is never finished knocking on hearts. What in one season seems like an impenetrable hardness may melt into a tender willingness the next. Thus, I never label anyone as *ultimately* resistant. That would refute God's sovereign, tenderizing work. However, in seasons of genuine resistance to healing, strugglers need to know several things.

First, there is no biblical basis for ordained homosexual relationships. Any attempt to distort Scripture or the witness of the Holy Spirit to reinforce one's homosexual practices needs to be deemed utterly false. It arises out of the creature's deception and sin. In no way should Christians ever concede to the pro-gay claim that the Creator blesses homosexual practices.

Second, those who actively pursue homosexual relationships should be barred from any kind of responsible position in the church until they renounce such practices and seek help. By *help* I mean real, ongoing accountability, counseling and whatever healing opportunities are available (for example, healing prayer, therapy and support groups [see Exodus referral address and telephone number in back]).

Third, those in the church who are practicing homosexual behavior should be treated no differently from any other sexual sinners. The same admonishment and discipline that apply to the heterosexual fornicator should apply to those engaged in homosexual practices—no more, no less. It's unjust to lower the standard of sexual purity for heterosexual singles but raise it up high for homosexual strugglers who have lovers or an addictive cycle of homosexual behavior. Sexual purity applies as stringently to those with heterosexual tendencies as it does to those struggling homosexually.

Be consistent. Don't magnify same-sex promiscuity simply because heterosexual sin seems more normal. That attitude may actually contribute to the stigma assigned to homosexuality. The church often closes its eyes to the inevitable undercurrent of heterosexual sin in its midst—pornography, addiction, fornication, sexual game-playing, compulsive masturbation. In turn the homosexual sinner, once exposed, becomes the scapegoat for the "normal" brokenness that is rarely confessed.

In that respect, homosexuals' willingness to confess their struggles and seek freedom may depend in part on the values and attitudes around them. Do church members confess their faults and failures to one another? Does one uphold for the other a word of encouragement and a vision of wholeness that enable him to walk uprightly? In short, is Christ's law fulfilled in the church by bearing one another's burdensome sins and weaknesses (see Gal. 6:1-2)?

A fellow pastor brought this point home for me. He described a church service after which he decided to act on his discernment that two members in attendance were gay. He called them into his office, and they both admitted their homosexuality and their status as lovers. The pastor kindly but firmly told them that each needed to repent of his sin and break off his relationship with the other. The one man replied: "You're not asking me to stop smoking or change my hair color. You're asking me to lay down everything I know to be true and tangible and submit myself to this Jesus and His church where I hardly know anybody, really. You're asking me to die.''

Alive to the spiritual metaphor of death unto new life, the pastor's eyes twinkled, and he replied almost merrily, ''That's exactly what I'm asking you to do.''

The man responded immediately, ''No one in this church has been called and held accountable to that kind of death. Don't start with me.'' With that, the two left and never returned.

While willingness is each person's individual responsibility, that willingness is awakened and enabled by the Holy Spirit who prepares each heart through a confessing, restorative community. I know of a handful of practicing strugglers who have come to the Vineyard and remained on the periphery due to their life-style, then eventually dropped out. Still others have come through Desert Stream and later realized they wanted to pursue homosexuality more than Jesus. But a solid number begin on the edge, uncertain of who Jesus is and who they are in light of Him, sexually and otherwise. Slowly but surely, the Lord woos them to Himself and His wholeness through worship, through pastors who convey God's order as well as their own vulnerabilities in living out that order, and through small groups where members genuinely want to know and be known by others, and where the confession of sin and forbearance of ongoing need is a given.

All these factors combine to awaken a willingness to be free from homosexuality. One by one, individuals like Jim come to me or another staff member and seek help. In light of the trust, security and truth the greater body has helped establish, strugglers are freed to be healed at a deeper, more risky level.

The Pain of Confession

How does this willingness to be free express itself? What does it mean to be repentant over one's homosexuality? The answer is threefold, and the first two responses involve a willingness to feel pain.

The first work of repentance is a willingness to be vulnerable, to confess that "this is a real problem that is really mine and that I cannot resolve on my own." Such vulnerability requires coming out of denial, the hiddenness that insists we remain in the dark and try to sort out the problem using our own limited resources. Often that denial has resulted in a double life: good Christians on one hand, raging homosexuals on the other. We may even reframe the darkness as light, or at least as an acceptable gray, to appease the pain of our own deception. Time after time, I have heard the confession of Christian men and women alike whom I knew reasonably well but who remained in denial about their need for healing for years, even decades. Addictive sexual behavior and emotionally broken relationships marked their lives. But shame and pride convinced them to stay silent about their homosexual feelings.

Such a confession is a monumental and painful step for such strugglers. It's monumental because it means stepping out of the false security of an image that's been carefully projected to others, an image that doesn't include what is, in fact, destroying them. The pain involved should be obvious. They feel naked without the "fig leaf" of deception. They become truly known—not only for wholeness and accomplishment, but for brokenness and intense struggle as well. In the gaze of spouses, friends, pastors or counselors, strugglers face themselves honestly. The insidious evil of their battle comes into the light. With their confession and cry for help, they admit they cannot and have not resolved it on their own.

The next step may be even more difficult. It involves turning from the controlling attitude of "Well, now that I've confessed my struggle, fix me. I don't want to struggle anymore. Take away my pain." When we will to be free and submit the brokenness at hand to Jesus and His people, the pain has just begun. The wearisome pain of deception eases, but in its place is the pain that lies at the core of the homosexual struggle. The pain of rejection and deprivation, of abuse, of loneliness, of the anxiety built by years of feeling alienated within and without—that which we have tried to ease again and again through homosexual pursuits—this is the pain Jesus wants to get at in order to heal the heart.

Repentance, then, involves turning to Jesus and others and saying, "Do what you need to do to help me get free." We no longer try to control how we'll be helped and how much pain we will or won't feel. And Jesus is faithful to walk with us as the painful issues arise, gently upholding us in the new and frightening journey of facing what was and is real in our lives.

Karen exemplifies this work of repentance. She had to come out of denial of her homosexual struggle and into recognition of her real pain and need for healing. Prior to her confession, she had been emotionally self-contained. It was as if she existed in the body of Christ only to serve and build up others; her needs were rarely apparent. She wrote off the healing of deeper inner needs and insight related to the soul as worldly and needless. The pain in her life was dismissed as irrelevant and as having been crucified with Christ. But her theological defense against inner healing was only a smoke screen for the deep fear she had of being out of control. Emotional vulnerability frightened her to death; it connoted the threat of emotional and sexual abuse and the awful lesbian craving she had suppressed for years. Karen would rather have led a missionary team in Kenya than confess her pain to another.

That's why her relationship with Susan was so powerful. The years of denial caught up with Karen. When someone attractive came into her life, she was almost powerless to withstand the temptation due to the overwhelming needs that had known so few constructive outlets. Facing the relationship and its end, Karen had to meet her greatest challenge. Did she really want to be whole? That meant, was she willing to come out of denial and allow people to see her for who she really was? Was she willing to submit her whole soul to Jesus and others and not control the healing process? For Karen and many like her, repenting means saying yes to those two questions.

Laying Down Homosexual Practices

But there's a second dimension to the willingness that leads to repentance: naming and laying down homosexual practices with the help of Jesus and others. These practices include homosexual relationships, romantic same-sex relationships that generate a homosexual bonding without being overtly erotic, anonymous homosexual encounters, use of homosexual pornography, and compulsive fantasy and masturbation.

All those things are efforts at grasping hold of same-sex love, or at least an image or sensation that gratifies one's longing. And at the core they are attempts at easing the pain of loneliness, at seeking to cover the naked, deprived parts of one's soul. The homosexual impulse, once conceived, becomes a way of meeting one's needs for intimacy, for reward, for pleasure, for a point of identification. But God demands that those who want to be free forsake the broken efforts of self-covering. Failure to try and do so signals an ultimate lack of willingness. It is false to say, ''I want to be free,'' but not to seek to lay down the false freedom of homosexual behavior.

I realize that homosexual relationships and addictive behavior don't cease to be a struggle simply because they're named as sin and repented of. People can will to change and still be in the throes of hard-earned victory marked by intermittent failures. But they must agree with God's heart and will to be free. That involves getting the support and accountability they need and *remaining* accountable. It means seeking God's heart toward the sin, permitting its grievous nature to sink down into the soul until they have an accurate grasp on the devastation wrought by it.

On a more positive note, the will to change means gaining momentum toward victory based upon God's true sexual intention for humanity. God wants to meet our needs aright. In turn He calls us to repent and sober up when we're engaged in false, destructive ways of meeting our needs.

Let me illustrate personally. At the beginning of this chapter, I described briefly my struggle with pornography during the course of my marriage and directorship of Desert Stream. The powerful and insidious nature of the material caught me off guard. For a period longer than I like to admit (approximately two years), I found myself caught up in a repetitive pursuit of mild pornographic material that resulted in masturbation. I would confess, but I still hung onto the prospect of release afforded me by pornography. My efforts at submitting the struggle to Jesus and others were sporadic. More often than not, I would return to the safe, isolated world of pornographic fantasy. I became addicted because of my gut-level unwillingness to grasp hold of the help available in the form of supportive, empowering friends.

One friend said to me, ''Your struggle is basically one of

control. You like the control pornography affords you. You would rather dive into that than take the risk of real intimacy.'' His words pierced like a sword. I *did* want control over how I found pleasure, and I didn't want to risk the prospect of not getting my needs met by real people.

I had to face Jesus in a sober way and allow the whole picture of my sin to hit me. I was bound; I needed to get real with myself, God and others and lay down the habit. God challenged me to obedience, insisting that I straighten up from that bent, addictive posture. Conviction struck in a way it hadn't before, and I began to resist the temptation at hand.

Through the support of my wife and friends and daily yielding to the Lord, the cycle was broken. I failed at times. I honestly felt pain when choosing not to cover myself in the shadowy images of pornography. But in responding to the Lord's call and getting the human support I needed, I began to get free. God empowered my will. And the result has been a new freeing up of positive, life-giving affection for my wife and friends.

I found that what I needed was *real* intimacy, *real* pleasure gained by communing with others. I also discovered that God wanted to strengthen me at a deeper level. Beneath the pornography habit lay an often-frightened, unaffirmed male who badly needed the encouragement of his Father. The demands of seminary, ministry and a new family had overwhelmed me. But instead of seeking cover in the truth of His powerful affirmation, I sought it in deception. Now, having broken that veil of deception and having relinquished a false way of meeting my needs, I am freed to receive what I really need.

Adopting the Higher Allegiance

That brings me to the third dimension of true repentance.

Having become vulnerable to one's powerlessness and pain, and having sought to lay down false ways of covering the pain and need, strugglers need to align themselves with the Lord. That means placing trust and allegiance in Him, going the way of the cross, holding fast to the Father when they feel like dying due to the loss of the safe and familiar. Jesus said to His disciples: "If anyone would come after me, he must deny himself and take up his cross daily and follow me. For whoever wants to save his life will lose it, but whoever loses his life for me will save it. What good is it for a man to gain the whole world, and yet lose or forfeit his very self?" (Luke 9:23-25).

Following Jesus means placing one's trust and hope wholly in Him. It means divesting oneself of broken and defensive ways of finding an identity and seeking only to identify with Him. A life blurred by broken habits and relationships is unable to discover the clarity and surety of being that comes through wholehearted allegiance to Jesus. To find one's true self, one must forsake all falsehood and follow Jesus.

This allegiance involves a fundamental realignment of the will. And it's usually a painful, sobering decision that each individual must make alone. Others are vital in helping the struggler come to the point of decision and in supporting him afterward. But no one can make the decision for the struggler. Each must genuinely face Jesus at that place where homosexual temptations and hopes loom larger than life. Whom will one serve, Jesus or the powerful lure of homosexual desire? One must bravely face one's options, then decide.

For Jim, this decision came after he had been a Christian for a year or so. He loved Jesus but also faced daily the lesser loves of homosexual addiction. Having grown weary of the tension of living between two worlds, which would he choose? Misery, not moral excellence, drove him to the decision. When he was ready, Jim chose to move out of his West Hollywood apartment. He moved in with a couple of guys from church and channeled his energies toward pursuing Jesus in prayer, Bible study and fellowship. Soon after, he received help from Desert Stream.

At times, Jim was incredibly lonely. Although he loved his roommates, both were detached and, for the most part, unable to uphold him in his struggle. He loved the church, but it took a long time to feel at home there. But he loved Jesus. And when trials came and threatened to throw him off course, Jim sought Him. The One to whom he had committed himself and his sexuality upheld Jim in those gray periods. With each experience of yielding to Jesus, trust developed. Jim learned to listen for His word, and he heard it through Scripture and the utterances of the Holy Spirit. Thus God strengthened Jim's decision to follow Him.

The same thing occurred for Karen. As we left her in stage one of the repentance process, she faced the challenge of letting go of a lesbian lover. This was especially difficult for her, because letting go meant being naked again, only this time with the memory of what it was like to be covered by another human being. Karen was extremely vulnerable. But in submitting that vulnerability to Jesus and committing herself to Him wholeheartedly, she entered into a new and dynamic level of reliance upon Him. For the first time, she met the true lover of her soul.

For both Karen and Jim, choosing Jesus over homosexual options, placing their hope and trust in Him, led to the maturing of their faith. Jesus became alive to them. He taught them to seek Him first and He prompted them to seek out the help of others, giving grace to those who were ineffective, even hurtful, in their care. He helped center them in the realization that He Himself is the reason for not giving up. He is the hope!

The degree to which one feels homosexually, the extent to which one's expectations of healing are met or not—these are not the fundamentals of faith. Jesus Himself is the hope. And in the process of becoming whole, strugglers are called to make firm their ultimate allegiance to Him. In good feelings and bad, in times of victory and defeat, Jesus wills that we *will* undivided loyalty to Him. That commitment is central to pressing into a deeper level of healing.

SIX

The Strength That Delivers

At the outset of Desert Stream, I spent a day with a very nice-looking guy who, in the course of our time together, acted seductively toward me. I loved it. I wasn't repulsed or morally outraged; a part of me would have thoroughly enjoyed having sex with him.

All I could do in light of my greater commitment to God and His work, as well as to Annette, was to remove myself forcibly and awkwardly from the situation and the man. But that night I wrestled with lust and the temptation to call him more than I had ever struggled before.

The occasion passed, but in retrospect I see the Lord was

using it to test me. Had I fallen, He could have forgiven me. But He could not have entrusted me with a ministry or a wife. From that day forward I held no illusion about my absolute safety from seducing or being seduced. Satan, the enemy, knew my vulnerability and was waging a war against me. I needed to be aware of his devices and even more alive to the gracious covering of my Father.

Satan also tried to defeat my ministry at its inception by discouraging me to the point of giving up. I walked into the home of a prominent group member and found him in bed with another. A mentally ill member assaulted a fellow struggler with lewd, abusive phone calls. My authority was continually challenged.

Often I would leave the meetings and ask the Lord on the way home, ''Why am I doing this?'' He responded, ''Do you love Me?'' I conceded. ''Then feed My sheep.'' He made it clear that this was *His* ministry to those oppressed by homo-sexuality. That took the burden off me and compelled me to seek Him as the Lord and sustainer—the bedrock strength—of the ministry.

Standing against the flesh and the devil requires divine strength, and allegiance to Jesus is key to being empowered by Him. The reason is simple. One whose focus on Jesus is undivided has more ready access to Him. The true heart knows that everything of genuine importance must come from Him. The power of lust and emotional dependency fails to master it. Instead the faithful heart seeks only the power of good—being mastered by Jesus.

Karen and Jim came to this point of seeking Jesus first. It took time. But in making firm their allegiance to Him, both began to experience an inner strength that had previously eluded them. Jim had never defined himself as ''strong.'' His self-image was composed more of labels and experiences that connoted passivity tending toward defeat, not victory.

Karen had always considered herself a strong woman, but of late she had come to question the depth of her power. Much of it had been a defense against the brokenness within. As the Lord tenderized her heart, she saw how much she needed genuine intimacy—love that entered the broken places inside and touched her. The Lord met her there and granted her His power.

For both Karen and Jim, this strength came through the person of the indwelling Holy Spirit. He had already entered into each heart at the point of receiving Jesus. But until the decision to obey Him had been made, the experience of His indwelling presence was erratic and grievously weakened by the dual allegiance to both Christianity and homosexuality. Now, with their wills aligned to Jesus, the real power of God could deepen in them.

That power is crucial to enabling the will to be free. We need a strength greater than our own! The amazing aspect of God's power as released in us through the Holy Spirit is that it enters our humanity and ignites the latent resources of power we have always possessed. They may be under-developed and weak, especially our choice-making faculties and our ability to say no to the immediate pleasure of sin. But God empowers our allegiance to the good. We know beyond a shadow of doubt that we are not alone in our struggle to be free. He who is greater pours Himself into the deepest recesses of our humanity and joins with us.

A New Base of Strength

Each struggler needs a new base out of which to operate, a reference point where true strength dwells. The writer of Hebrews described Jesus as "an anchor for the soul, firm and secure" (Heb. 6:19). Paul prayed that God would ''strengthen you with power through his Spirit in your inner being'' (Eph. 3:16) and went on to describe how the Holy Spirit roots and grounds us in love Himself (see Eph. 3:17-19). The Spirit, then, grants us a profound assurance of God's advocacy. Not only can we know about the Creator in all His awesome power, but He even stands with us, in us, upholding us in His power. That power has life-changing implications for the homosexual struggler.

Jim had labored most of his life under the shadow of his perceived powerlessness. In athletics, in peer relationships and at home with his father, he felt inadequate, unable to break through a vague sense of not being good enough. He developed a subtle kind of helplessness. Throughout adolescence and early adulthood, he would bow out in the face of conflictual relationships and situations and move on to something less threatening. He had little sense of what it meant to conquer the fear inherent in life's challenges. Instead he avoided those challenges to protect himself from failure.

His homosexual struggles were another expression of his broken view of self. It wasn't until He accepted Jesus and dealt forthrightly with his problem that he realized he could change his life. Desires within and temptations without threatened to ensnare him. But as he learned to rely on Jesus and to hold true to that greater desire, Jim became aware of the real strength within him.

During a prayer time together, I asked God to strengthen him through His Spirit. We waited and asked the Father to grant clarity to Jim about the measure of His strength indwelling him.

Before too long, Jim received a memory of playing baseball at school. Not being a good player, he had struck out and was humiliated by several teammates who called him a ''faggot,'' ''woman'' and other emasculating terms. Jim had slouched off to right field while the other team came to bat. Fighting back tears, he now perceived the Lord entering the memory and upholding him. Jesus stood with him and encouraged him. He expressed anger at his rejecters, and with the Lord's help he refused to grant them the satisfaction of seeing him quit. Instead he aligned himself with the greater power of Jesus and stood tall. He became alive to the game once more. The experience profoundly testified to Jim about Jesus' strength *in him* as a source of courage and perseverance. In his vulnerability to rejection in traditionally masculine activities, he received Jesus as a much-needed ally.

After the prayer time I made it clear to Jim that exercising his empowered will was a key to the liberation of greater strength in his life. One does not become empowered solely in isolation; that power becomes fully realized in battle.

A few days later, he suffered a major setback on the job. He had been working hard toward a promotion that his boss gave to someone else. Angry at himself, his boss and the whole frustrating situation, he stuffed his real feelings and got depressed. In that detached, self-pitying place, he hungered for the masculine images in pornography and decided to obtain some after leaving the office. While Jim drove to the adult bookstore, however, Jesus jogged his memory. He brought home the truth that Jim didn't need a false fix of the masculine; He Himself was the source of the affirming, powerful love he needed, and that power was alive and well in his own heart.

He resisted the realization at first. But when he considered the greater impotence he would experience following the use of pornography, he stopped. He pulled the car over and allowed the presence of Jesus to well up within him. He chose to align himself with that greater source of power, and Jesus affirmed his adequacy as a man. He helped him identify and convey the real anger he held toward his boss. Jim screamed out his frustration, then sobbed with disappointment. Jesus upheld him throughout, making clear to Jim that his boss didn't have the final say on his goodness as a man—He did.

With that, Jim drove home. He felt shaky but confident. He committed himself to having a good time with some friends that evening. Alive to the Lord's advocacy of his masculine will, Jim chose the real solution to his frustration, and he continues to exercise the newfound strength that Jesus has wrought in his life.

Karen's experience of her empowered will was a bit different. As already mentioned, Karen possessed a kind of strength already. But it wasn't born out of admitted need and vulnerability; her strength was a defense against those two things. Her empowering came when she finally confessed her need to another.

A few months after her breakup with Susan, Karen felt sorely tempted to reconnect with her. The mundane realities of her life, Christian and otherwise, slowly eroded the initial spark to obey. All she knew was her loneliness and the way Susan filled that need. She didn't feel like praying. All she could do was call a close friend from church, one of the few who knew of her struggle.

Sensing the battle Karen was in, Becky (the friend) went over to her house and prayed that the Lord's tender mercy and love would meet Karen in her longing. Karen could receive this, especially in light of the vision Jesus had given her as bridegroom to bride (described in chapter 4). As His love broke into her desire for Susan, Karen straightened up a bit. It was as if Jesus was enabling her to rise out of being ''bent'' (thanks to Leanne Payne's use of C.S. Lewis's imagery) toward Susan. Through the sensitive prayer of a solid, nonerotic friend, Karen, now upright before the Lord and receptive to Him, could receive His strength.

In prayer the Lord made it clear to Karen that He wanted to stand as the guard around her heart. He wanted to protect what went in and out of it. Given her newly realized neediness, Jesus wanted to be Lord over her desires and how she pursued their fulfillment. Could she trust Him for that? Karen agreed to do so, and Becky prayed that all thoughts and desires, especially related to Susan, would first have to be yielded to Jesus. In turn, incoming overtures from Susan and others would also need to encounter the cross. Karen welcomed His protection as she sought to walk in her new-found inner strength.

The Divine Paradox

The paradox here is that God's strength is realized upon the admission of weakness. In other words, the homosexual tendency becomes a channel of God's strength once submitted to Him. This is similar to Paul's boasting about the thorn in his flesh in 2 Corinthians 12:9-10. Here the apostle described why the Lord did not remove his thorn, or weakness: "He said to me, 'My grace is sufficient for you, for my power is made perfect in weakness.' Therefore I will boast all the more gladly about my weaknesses, so that Christ's power may rest on me. That is why, for Christ's sake, I delight in weaknesses, in insults, in hardships, in difficulties. For when I am weak, then I am strong."

As both Karen's and Jim's examples illustrate, their strong yearnings ceased to dominate them at the point of yielding the desires to the Lord. That act of the will, born of recognized vulnerability, inspired an awakening of the true and good that dwelled within—Jesus Himself.

That yielding of weakness resulting in strength can occur

in one's private communion with the Lord. Every struggler faces times of overwhelming weakness when no one else is around. In Jim's close call with pornography, for example, he had no option but to cry out to the Lord. But sometimes we need others to help mediate this process. Confession of weakness often needs to be received by brothers and sisters who are then ministers of divine strength. For example, Karen needed Becky's prayer; her heart and mind were muddled to the extent that it was difficult for her—maybe even impossible—to hear clearly from God directly. But she could make a phone call, and she could submit herself to a healthy other through whose presence she would receive that greater power of the Lord.

Not only does confession of weakness to a friend work, but it also keeps us rooted in the reality that we are relational beings who need others. We're also fallible people who are sorely tempted to hide our vulnerabilities. We can even use our spirituality to hide from others. Many of us react to our idolatrous, dependent patterns in homosexuality by swinging to an extremely individual quest for God. We don't want our walk with Him sullied by potential brokenness in our Christian relationships.

But Jesus insists on the reality that we are human beings, created "not to be alone" and compelled to work out our salvation by allowing others to know our weaknesses and in turn strengthen us in them. He calls out His true image in us through His witness in the image of a brother or sister. That keeps us rooted on earth and not in spiritual abstractions. Most important, it enables Jesus to strengthen us in a way that unites us in love with others, as well as with Himself. Bonhoeffer wrote about this poignantly in *Life Together*:

> God has willed that we should seek and find His living Word in the witness of a brother, in the mouth

of a man. Therefore, the Christian needs another Christian who speaks God's Word to him. He needs him again and again when he becomes uncertain and discouraged, for by himself he cannot help himself without belying the truth. He needs his brother man as bearer and proclaimer of the divine word of salvation. He needs his brother solely because of Jesus Christ. The Christ in his own heart is weaker than the Christ in the word of his brother; his own heart is uncertain, his brother's is sure (p. 23).

The Reality of Evil

Yet even with the help of fellow believers, the struggle continues. For in spite of Christ's victory in us, neither sin nor Satan has been totally dethroned. Jesus broke the ultimate power of both. But in the current age, between Calvary and Christ's second coming, Satan seeks to dominate us still and will stop at nothing to hook into our vulnerabilities and destroy us with them. In other words, homosexual strugglers must contend with evil. Satan has a great deal invested in sexual brokenness, homosexuality included. If strugglers want to be truly free, they must be willing to face squarely the enemy's hand in their trials. In turn, battle plans must be made and effectively exercised. In granting us His power, Jesus calls us to fight!

Grasping the truth about Satan's hand in sexual brokenness first involves reaffirming the original intention of sexuality, the motivation to seek union with another in body, soul and spirit and thus ease our aloneness. But heterosexual covenant involves more than meeting the needs of God's human creation; it also reveals His heart. God's image shines forth in whole heterosexual relating.

97

God's image is also expressed in terms of marital fidelity. His commitment to His people and His desire for their commitment are symbolized by the faithful heterosexual covenant. Throughout Scripture, especially in the Old Testament, God's fidelity to His people is compared to the faithfulness of husband to wife. God committed Himself to Israel; He wooed and wed her. He promised His faithfulness and asked her in turn to be faithful to Him.

The analogy works in the opposite direction as well. The utterly hallowed nature of God's making covenant with His people extends to God's commitment to the marital covenant. He indwells and blesses that covenant, and under that blessing, sexual yearning and erotic expression find a haven for powerful release. Further, Scripture offers the relationship between husband and wife as an analogy to Christ's relationship with the church (see Eph. 5:25-33).

But if the power of sexuality within a marital covenant reflects the power of God's commitment to mankind, broken sexuality reveals spiritual darkness and grieves His heart. It casts a shadow on who He is and on how He wants to love His people and be loved by them. We see this throughout Scripture. God symbolized Israel's unfaithfulness with the imagery of adultery, and that unfaithfulness was revealed by the immoral sexual practices in which she engaged. The care and purity with which the Israelites maintained appropriate sexual boundaries were a good indication of the nation's spiritual health. And immoral relations rendered her indistinguishable from surrounding nations and their vast array of pagan deities.

Israel's allegiance to other gods divided her heart and weakened her spiritual immune system. She therefore ran the risk of growing sick and apathetic. Increasingly numb to her covenant with God, Israel became demonized. Spiritual darkness shrouded her pursuit of idols and the accompanying sexually immoral practices. The prophet Jeremiah decried this repeatedly. As God's spokesman, he called out to the nation, "You have scattered your favors to foreign gods under every spreading tree, and have not obeyed me" (Jer. 3:13). "The people of Judah...have set up their detestable idols in the house that bears my Name and have defiled it" (Jer. 7:30). "You have forgotten me and trusted in false gods. I will pull up your skirts over your face that your shame may be seen— your adulteries and lustful neighings, your shameless prostitution!" (Jer. 13:25-27).

In her disobedience to Yahweh, Israel set up altars to Baal in the form of wooden phallic images and made food offerings to Ashteroth, goddess of the earth. The nation's landscape was marked by these testaments to spiritual and sexual brokenness:

> Surely the idolatrous commotion on the hills and mountains is a deception; surely in the Lord our God is the salvation of Israel. From our youth shameful gods have consumed the fruit of our father's labor— their flocks and herds, their sons and daughters. Let us lie down in our shame, and let our disgrace cover us. We have sinned against the Lord our God, both we and our fathers; from our youth till this day we have not obeyed the Lord our God (Jer. 3:23-25).

Baal and Ashteroth were Canaanite fertility gods. Both represented the "natural" cycles of life, yet neither acknowledged Yahweh—the Creator and sustainer of nature. These gods mediated the worship of the sun, of reproduction, of the harvest—the rhythms of life. Unlike Yahweh, who was worshipped as the holy "Other," Baal and Ashteroth were experienced through release of one's own sensual desires.

Their worship digressed to highly charged eroticism. Somehow, an offering was made to these fertility gods through illicit orgasm.

But Baal and Ashteroth weren't real gods at all. Both were satanic counterfeits that snatched sexuality from the hands of the Creator, reduced it to eroticism, and propped up that eroticism as the object of worship. Submission to these gods meant bowing the knee to the demonic principalities of sexual perversion. In effect, idealized, eroticized images of the creature were being worshipped, and worship degenerated into nothing more than orgies. The collision of body parts between faceless, nameless people marked the depths of Israel's idolatry. (For more information on the role of spiritual darkness in broken sexuality, please see *Pursuing Sexual Wholeness* guidebook, chapters 5 and 15.)

Modern Idolatry

What does Israel's spiritual and sexual idolatry have to do with us today? *Plenty.* Whenever anyone, Christian or not, yields his body to another for erotic gratification outside the heterosexual covenant, he makes a sacrifice to Baal. The principality of sexual perversion is alive and well. We bow down to it whenever we engage in sexual immorality. We may not mouth prayers to Baal or Ashteroth, but we worship them with each illicit orgasm, each immoral fantasy, each pornographic watch we keep, each seductive, controlling gesture.

The enemy of our souls pays special attention to our sexual vulnerabilities. He knows well the power of inspired sexuality to reveal God and His faithful provision. He knows, too, the devastation wrought by perversion—how it obscures our true selves and competes powerfully with our first-love commitment to Christ. So Satan longs to belittle and constrain us with sexual perversion. He weds himself to our inner vulnerability, empowers sin's conception, then becomes the lord of this new expression of perversion, delighting in its dominating effects on us, his subjects. He helps us nurture the perversion, seeking to destroy our allegiance to Jesus, leading us into an eternity in hell.

Satan especially delights in homosexual perversion because it not only exists outside of marriage, but it also defiles God's very image reflected as male and female. That's why Paul used homosexual behavior as an *extreme* symbol of the sexual perversion that results from spiritual idolatry (see Rom. 1:18-32). Accordingly, Satan knows that if he can render strugglers hopeless in the face of their tendencies and bound in their pursuit of same-sex love, he has woven a thick and binding idolatrous thread into the fabric of that Christian's life.

That demonic commitment to the sameness inherent in homosexuality is apparent in isolated groups of male and female strugglers. The enemy delights in veiled flirtations and seductive cues exchanged in such a context. Those who have yet to yield to such subtleties often find themselves ensnared by this unspoken network of homosexual desires.

The enemy perpetuates one major myth in this context—the sense of gender superiority: we, the same, are superior to you, the other. This is especially true in lesbianism. Although not often defined as such, female strugglers congregate with each other on the basis of the perceived superiority of a woman's capacity to love and be loved. Such an attitude, often born of hurt and perpetuated by deceptive experience, keeps women mired in dependent same-sex relationships. In effect, these relationships are ruled by the evil one, who indwells and plays upon the rebellion against God's order.

The reason for Satan's indwelling the lust for sameness

is obvious. Without the presence of men in the tight group of lesbian strugglers, light and objectivity that are distinctly masculine cannot inform the dark, enmeshed patterns of relating that can occur, often with the women oblivious to any hazards.

Kathy, a good friend intent on overcoming lesbian patterns in her own life, described to me a situation that illustrates this well. She got together with a group of old female friends, all Christians with homosexual tendencies, who for the most part had never dealt with the core issues related to their lesbianism. Over the course of their time together, Kathy found herself caught up in the sexual energy at hand. She wanted to be seen as a tough yet feminine object of desire, and she began to posture herself in a way that was at once an assertion of strength *and* seductive intent. She partook of, but felt uncomfortable with, the amount of touching going on between the women: backrubs and long, intimate hugs. Kathy even felt jealous toward one of the women whom she perceived was getting more attention than she was getting.

After the evening was over, Kathy felt spiritually "slimed." She had come under the principality of homosexual perversion that intensifies in group settings. Together, the women hovered around the edges of Baal worship, and they found no release because of the same-sex enclave they created in defense against the masculine.

Kathy took action: she organized a party involving these women and invited an equal number of men. The group was small enough to prevent the women from walling off the men. According to Kathy, none of the broken, oppressive patterns emerged. The women were called out of their same-sex focus by the men. In the light of complementarity, the perverse striving for same-sex completion was checked.

Another, related source of demonization is the homosexual

relationship itself. The attempt to consummate a one-flesh union with a member of the same sex brings one immediately under the realm of Baal—the principalities of perversion. Many pro-gay Christians attempt to divorce the whole issue of gender from true spirituality in relationships. The Scripture does not give us that option. Gender complementarity reflects God's image! An attempt at same-sex consummation defiles that image. Thus, the union cannot be blessed by the Creator of the image, because that would defile His own creative purposes as set down in Scripture. Instead it comes under the domain of Satan himself.

For those in homosexual relationships, such an assessment may seem light years away from the good feelings of attachment and even a kind of spiritual communion that exists in the relationship. That attachment and communion are indeed inspired, but their source is demonic.

The deception is incredibly effective because of the power of sexual bonding. One genuinely *feels* release, belonging and covering. The warm, sensual acceptance of a lover seems to melt away decades of loneliness and alienation. The enemy knows the yearning and its seeming release. He knows the power of homosexual communion. And he will employ its sensual and emotional returns to deceive us mightily. Many solid Christians have rejected orthodox Christianity due to homosexual unions or, worse, have tried to conform orthodoxy to their deceived status. Once their wills are yielded to the sin, they submit their souls and spirits to the ravages of the evil one.

It should be clear by now that homosexual struggles are not merely soulish vulnerabilities. Satan, as the lord and perpetrator of all perversion, infuses those struggles with his power and provides lethal options for resolving them. And when we willfully violate the boundaries intended to protect us—sex within the confines of a committed heterosexual covenant—we open ourselves up to satanic oppression. Like the Israelites, we crowd the altar to Jesus in our hearts with an altar made to Baal.

Finding Deliverance

We must wake up to this spiritual reality if we're to battle against it. And the main tool of our warfare is the love of Jesus. As we learn to submit our struggles, our unmet needs, *our lives* to the mercy and compassion of Jesus, Satan must flee. Commitment to our heart's true desire liberates the mastery of lesser desires. We need His presence! We cannot get free of the darkness unless we're bathed in the light.

As we respond to that love by pledging our allegiance to *the rule of Christ Jesus*, we are delivered. By deliverance I don't mean being rid altogether of homosexual feelings. As we shall see, emotional and relational healing must occur alongside deliverance. But deliverance defined as ''the power of love purging the power of perversion'' frees the struggler all the more to grow in grace and truth. It rids one of the dominating, pervasive power of lust. God frees the struggler to rise up and take hold of Jesus in the face of temptation instead of slouching toward sin. The power of God is liberated in one's soul and will, freeing the struggler to choose Jesus and grow in His love.

Deliverance accompanies genuine repentance, the willingness to turn to Jesus, as we saw in the last chapter. Alive to the power of His love, strugglers renounce the perversion at hand. They assert Jesus as their strong man and allow the Holy Spirit to do His purging work. But they must also will to walk free from the objects of perversion or they may find themselves more bound than ever.

Terry, my good friend and counselee, once received a

powerful deliverance. A few years ago, some church members prayed for him and cast out several spirits that had empowered homosexual lust and crippled his faith. Afterward, Terry felt a tremendous change. For the first time, he began to say no to homosexual behavior. He also experienced a deepened joy and receptivity to Jesus.

One month later, however, Terry met a Christian man who became his lover. The relationship lasted only a few months, but the oppression that followed sent him into a spiritual and emotional tailspin that lasted three years. He finally bottomed out and sought help from Desert Stream.

A slow rebuilding process began. I refused to pray for Terry's deliverance until I had ascertained his willingness. When we finally did pray, we encountered a huge spiritual band around his heart. This band blocked Terry from receiving the love of Jesus. After his first deliverance, the enemy had anchored himself around Terry's heart using four key areas of disobedience: bitterness toward God, bitterness toward his family, his pornography addiction and his ongoing obsession with his former love. Until Terry was ready to repent and renounce these four areas, his heart would remain like stone.

I'm happy to say Jesus triumphed. As we prayed for him, Terry worshipped Jesus and wept for His lost love. The band loosened. Through my previous knowledge of Terry's struggle and the illumination of the Holy Spirit, the three other pray-ers and I identified the four cords Satan had used to bind Terry's heart. Jesus helped Terry to recognize the bitterness and the altars of Baal erected through his sexual fantasies and practices. Motivated by his hunger for Jesus, Terry repented and renounced all four sources of sin and bondage. And Jesus delivered his heart, freeing Terry to love Him.

Unlike the first deliverance, Terry soberly lived out this

one by staying on the alert for Satan's counterattack. Most important, he devoted himself to prayer and worship, realizing how much he had missed Jesus. Terry continues to grow in strength and confidence, though struggles remain. But one thing is clear: with the Holy Spirit's help, Terry will not allow the enemy to rob him a second time of the *Real*—Christ Jesus, the only true and steadfast lover of his soul.

Oppression related to homosexuality and other forms of sexual brokenness isn't always easy to discern, however. Satan's devices are varied and veiled; he loves to remain hidden. Sometimes he oppresses us through experiences we can hardly recall—our first exposure to pornography, early illicit sexual activity, the trauma of sexual abuse. A child's exposure to graphic expressions of adult sexuality seems to be a major access point to sexual oppression. Thus, deliverance prayer is aimed first at the point of initial access and proceeds from there.

Another powerful factor seems to be the sexual sins of our ancestors. When blood relatives who have gone before bowed down to Baal in the form of illicit sexual activities, we may be vulnerable to the same or similar oppression ourselves. (For more information on this, please read chapter 6 in the *Pursuing Sexual Wholeness* guidebook.) Many strugglers to whom I have ministered were spiritually disposed to sexual brokenness through the often hidden, unredeemed perversions of their forefathers.

In the Living Waters groups, we pray intently and thoroughly through each preceding generation unto the tenth. We also pray over each homosexual relationship and behavior pattern that lies in the struggler's history. (For a detailed description of breaking one-flesh unions, see chapter 9 of *Pursuing Sexual Wholeness* guidebook.) Given the individual's willingness, we agree with him as he repents of the sinful behavior or relationship, renounces the spiritual stronghold and then raises high the victory and lordship of Jesus in its stead. Many have received substantial freedom through this prayerful searching out of the various avenues through which the enemy had bound them sexually (more on this in chapter 5 of *Pursuing Sexual Wholeness* guidebook.)

Our Willingness, His Power

Deliverance from the demonic strongholds tied to sexual brokenness requires first our willingness and repentance. Then the Lord's powerful love enables the deliverance and frees us to receive more of Him. We learn to do spiritual battle as we come to discern the subtle oppression that can overtake us homosexually.

We looked earlier at the bondage of sameness that arises in unredeemed groups of strugglers and in gay relationships and practices. As we become yielded to Him in these areas, the Lord begins to sensitize us when we come under the authority of principalities of perversion.

I once had an experience in a dime store where I was surprised by a graphic display of hard-core pornography—an unexpected offering that assaulted me visually and spiritually. By God's grace, I immediately raised high the victory of Jesus over the principalities surrounding the material. I asserted His power and authority to dispel the evil one's purposes there, and I turned away untouched by the darkness.

Jesus wants us to stand in His strength and discernment in the face of our struggle. He calls us to battle the evil that seeks to attach itself to our sexual vulnerability. He wants to and *can* deliver us from the darkness, heal the brokenness in our souls and restore our sexuality to the Father's original intent.

SEVEN

Hope for Gender Wholeness

How does a person's gender identity get messed up? In my own childhood I received plenty of parental affirmation coupled with discipline. Yet that affirmation didn't give me a sense of being distinctly male. I remember from early on a consistent demarcation between my two elder brothers and my sister Jean and me. My brothers' combative, aggressive style put me off. In turn, my efforts to enter in as "one of the boys" frequently resulted in my being tagged a sissy.

Such rejection reinforced an increasingly profound sense of unworthiness as a male, as well as a perceived inability to compete and succeed on male turf. The "fighting" spirit of boyhood was nearly defeated in me before it had a chance to develop.

Instead I found quiet pursuits—domestic and artistic in contrast to competitive—more to my liking. Jean and I shared a room, friendships and feminine interests. Strong, loving women became role models at home and in the media. Old family films portray me as sweetly passive; in one frame I'm wearing nail polish. Don't get me wrong—I didn't believe myself to be a little girl. I simply gravitated toward the feminine because of its care and compassion, a redemptive contrast to the harsh and arbitrary manner I came to equate with the masculine. In other words, I knew myself to be a boy, but I didn't know strong and encouraging male relationships that helped call out and "bless" the little boy in me.

Granted, I probably wasn't an easy boy for many male peers and adults to bless. I preferred playing house to war, wielding a paint brush instead of a baseball bat. These preferences grew out of my personality and probably put off the more rough-and-tumble variety of males.

I hooked right into the cycle. With each rejecting, anxiety-producing encounter, I walled off a bit and became more cautious, and eventually caustic, toward them. Even those who were well-intentioned could be discounted. My lens became skewed toward me, my posture defensive. In trying to protect myself, I cut myself off from the good, life-affirming nutrients that males in my early life might have given.

Two instances may illustrate this. Once at age five, I and a neighborhood girl were playing with dolls when her older brother walked in and jeered. A couple of days later, he and his friends ridiculed me. I remember hurrying home in pain, alone, almost immobilized by feelings of shame and freakishness. I never fought back but I swallowed their rejection.

110

The result was hating them and myself and rejecting my maleness.

A few years later, in grade school, I recall walking about our schoolyard in abject fear of running into a small group of guys who were always accusing me of being a "woman," a homosexual, a sissy and so on. I felt defenseless in the face of their tauntings and ashamed of my powerlessness.

Where were my parents in all this? Dad was kind but low key, not a particularly strong presence. Like most dads, he was more busy on the job than emotionally invested at home. I also think he was a bit at a loss concerning how to be a catalyst for his family. He never had one when he was growing up.

In retrospect, I wish he had been *more present* for me. I needed a primary source of encouragement in the face of some major gaps in my gender identity. *I needed a male covering.* Unlike many sons, I'm sure, my somewhat cautious, sensitive nature necessitated that he come alongside me and stand with me in the challenge of charging into boyhood. As it was, my battle cry was more of a whimper.

Mom had invested more in me than Dad. And ironically, she would challenge me to stand up and "face the music" more than Dad would. I appreciated that. But she could take me only so far in blessing my male identity. And at times her input failed to clarify my dilemma.

I remember one confusing message from her. She walked in on me once while a male friend and I were playing dress up, with me in the female role. She told me that role-playing "Mommy" and "Daddy" could help me to be a better daddy when I grew up. Besides being a hard concept for a six-year-old to grasp, her response failed to consider my over-identification with the feminine.

That's where my parents' humanistic value system broke

111

down. The near abolition of gender differences and roles during the era of my childhood (in the 1960s) made it difficult for them to identify and possibly help remedy what was becoming a crisis in my gender identity and ultimately in my sexuality.

I'm aware of portraying a somewhat contradictory picture of my upbringing by describing good and bad aspects of my parents simultaneously. Yet that's reality. My father sought to be a strong covering for his family, yet I remained naked and vulnerable in my gender identity. My mother attempted to be that covering and couldn't. I don't blame my parents for the totality of my sexual struggle, but I don't discount their contribution to it, either. That parents have a remarkable effect on their children's identity (sexual and otherwise) is unquestionable. That such an influence can be reduced to simple cause-and-effect quotients is impossible due to the complex and subtle "dance" within which children either receive or resist the exchange of emotional nutrients from their parental partners. The third and most tragic option is to dance alone. Concerning my parents, I am grateful for their presence and mournful over the lack of connection with them in certain areas of my life, particularly that of my gender identity.

And gender is an awesome reality. The degree to which one has made peace with his maleness or her femaleness greatly affects personal wholeness. In particular, gender security is crucial for heterosexual relating. With a secure sense of one's maleness or femaleness, one naturally yearns for the other, the complement that can draw out and complete one's true self. Gender wholeness also reveals God's image, granting one the capacity to reflect Himself.

But if gender security liberates the true self, gender brokenness constrains it. By *brokenness* I mean an unaffirmed, possibly abused gender identity. Those in the throes of this brokenness may equate personal gender identity with anxiety and inadequacy. Not having measured up as men or women in the eyes of others, they detach from that vital part of themselves and become derailed along the track to whole relationships.

I realize gender is a sensitive issue, especially for those who have been "gender abused." Furthermore, the language used to describe true maleness and femaleness, as well as true masculinity and femininity, is awkward and subject to misinterpretation. But we must wrestle with these realities. God's image is reflected in the merging of true maleness and true femaleness. I believe as well that the Christian life can be aptly described as the complementary rhythm of the true feminine and true masculine. Believing both leads me to wrestle with the conclusion that gender realities are somehow rooted in God and His creation. Gender isn't merely a cultural prescription; it's essential to all people in every culture who seek to reveal God in their personal identity and relationships.

Those with homosexual tendencies help us to understand better the significant role of gender in one's sexuality and spirituality. In their histories and current fears, strugglers often reveal to us the grave problems that arise out of an un-affirmed gender identity. We also catch a glimpse of what that brokenness looks like, as well as the revelation of gender wholeness as it emerges over the course of one's journey out of homosexuality.

The Importance of Gender

Jim lived most of his life out of touch with the goodness of his masculinity. From as far back as he could recall, he resented being a boy. More than not, he felt inadequate in sports and in the rowdy activity of the boys around his neighborhood. Their rejection of him led him further to disavow the masculine. He came to equate masculinity with abusive power.

His father reinforced that perspective. Jim recalls his father's frustration with him for not being a better athlete, a tougher competitor. His dad also couldn't relate very well to his aptitude in art and academics. Many conversations occurred with his dad that left Jim feeling inadequate and bound. On the one hand, he really wanted to measure up to the boys. On the other hand, he didn't perceive in himself the strength and courage to rise to the occasion alone. Tragically, his father was not his advocate in the journey toward manhood. He was more like a larger version of Jim's peers, chastening him for not being "man enough" but not enabling Jim to get in touch with that strength.

Jim entered adolescence with an oppressive shadow over his personhood. Alienated from his male peers and his own sense of masculine adequacy, he felt crippled in his capacity to forge an identity and sense of purpose. To make matters worse, he became aware of intense homosexual yearnings. What was happening to Jim became clear to him later on. Split off from his strength and adequacy as a young man, as well as the life-giving power of his maturing body and sexuality, Jim was vulnerable to attempting to gain that masculine power by possessing one who seemingly embodied it. (Special thanks to Leanne Payne for her invaluable insights on "cannibal compulsion." See *The Broken Image*, pp. 149-50, and chapter 9 of *Pursuing Sexual Wholeness* guidebook.)

Jim knew none of this in his conscious mind. Nevertheless, the long stretches of deprivation and anxiety underlying his weakened sense of gender had taken their toll. He didn't know who he was as a man; no bridge existed over which he could cross into the certainty of his masculine adequacy. In an effort to discover that certainty, he sought the masculine through homosexual feelings and fantasies.

But Jim's subconscious attempt at bolstering his gender identity was fallen. His real need wasn't erotic. Another man's genitals or well-developed physique couldn't confirm Jim's gender adequacy. Jim needed to become alive to his own power and adequacy. And having become awakened to his masculinity, he needed to make friends with it. In so doing, the *quality* of masculinity could become rooted in his maleness.

Let me elaborate a bit. Maleness involves the state of being a man instead of a woman. It's directly tied to one's biological gender. Masculinity is a quality, a posture, an approach to life that is complemented by femininity. Men and women alike will express both feminine and masculine qualities over the course of their lifetimes. But to be whole men and women, those qualities must find a harmony and a rhythm that is appropriate to their biological sex.

Jim's example may help us to understand this. As a child, Jim embraced the feminine. He didn't embrace ''femaleness,'' as he always considered himself male. But his posture toward life was one of gentle receptivity. He preferred quiet conversation and domestic games over more rough-and-tumble activities. He would freeze in the face of conflict with other boys and retreat into the pages of a book or within the safety of his own home, where female friends and he could play. He embraced the power of deep feeling and the capacity to draw meaning out of what life offered, especially in terms of significant relationships, and he approached life cautiously.

But that profound feminine capacity failed to help him make peace with the masculine realities within and outside himself. The ability to initiate, to effect change, to fight and lose and fight again, to relish the prospect of victory and push through every resistance until it's achieved, to take one's deeply held emotions and convictions and act upon them—this is the masculine rhythm that eluded Jim. As already described in brief, Jim cowered in the face of the often-brutal expressions of masculinity that he perceived in his peers and his father, and he withdrew into the feminine.

In this way, even the feminine turned false; it failed him as he grew older. Jim couldn't build a life on deep, increasingly dark feelings; he couldn't sustain whole relationships when captivated by intense homosexual urges. The goodness of true friendship was trampled by the edgy, compulsive nature of his sexuality. He lived life off-center, detached from the real masculine and bent toward false expressions of masculinity that promised release but only belittled his already broken sense of self.

Jim's story is similar to that of many men who struggle homosexually. Unaffirmed in their masculinity and afraid of it, they become disoriented in their maleness. It's as if true masculinity needs to be awakened in them. Conversely, they have a solid base of the true feminine—the capacity to receive the truth about themselves and rise up in it. The stage is set for wholeness.

This is unlike many heterosexual men who live life out of a broken, imbalanced sense of masculinity. Having never made peace with feminine ways of knowing and perceiving, they spend much of their lives resisting the feminine. These men can seduce women but cannot commit to them and love them. They can win a football game but cannot carry on an intimate conversation. They can do a lot of things but don't know how simply to be—in relationships, before the Lord, with themselves. The result can be a restless, agitated approach to life in which deeper meaning and values are rarely savored. Such drivenness is its own form of gender brokenness: men alive to masculine power whose hearts wither. Without the true feminine, men cannot be whole.

Women with lesbian tendencies face a similar dilemma. Cut off from the feminine, their femaleness fails to become whole. But unlike men, who don't face the task of making peace with their femaleness, women must. Flight from the feminine will mean a crippled capacity to resolve who they are as women and may also express itself in a yearning for union with another woman. Karen's history illustrates this.

Karen grew up with a mother who was immature and un-affirmed in her own right. She had married young, and early on in her marriage she faced the hard realities of a household full of mundane responsibilities and a husband who no longer loved her. She also relied on her daughter inordinately as a sounding board for her woes.

The response from Karen was mixed. On the one hand, she loved her mother and wanted to help her. On the other hand, she resented her mom's neediness and stopped re-specting her. Her mother gave her a broken picture of femininity. To be feminine meant powerlessness, being burdened down with the needs of others without one's own being considered. That became even more apparent when Karen's mother found out about her husband's long-standing affair with another woman. Karen came to believe that femininity meant submission leading to despair.

This wasn't the humble posture that God or anyone else could exalt; it was the posture of victimization. She hated her mother for such impotence, hated her own feelings of powerlessness and vulnerability, and vowed never to be trapped by this perception of femininity.

Karen was in a hard place. She wanted a man but couldn't trust him. Several early, abusive experiences with teenage dates sealed her mistrust. She viewed most of her female peers as frivolous and silly. And she hungered for love, a love inspired in part by the lack of intimate care and protection afforded her by her parents during her early life.

In a way, Karen had not been mothered. Her mom had been a kind of older friend who seemed to need her as much as Karen needed a mother. The little girl within Karen longed to be held and protected. Much of this yearning was called forth by women who seemingly possessed strength as well as feminine beauty. But as soon as those feelings arose, she squelched them on the grounds that they were weak and risky. She continued in her own strength, burying her need for love and compensating for it by becoming more strong, more competent, more successful in her faith and her career.

But she was locked into her crisis in gender identity. She continued to resist most women because of their impotence and most men because of their abusiveness. And unknowingly, she was greatly at odds with herself. Her body, her sexuality, her need for intimacy and connection became cut off from her mind and will. That was obvious in her drab, genderless appearance. She wore baggy, outdated clothes and carried herself rigidly. Split off from the real feminine, Karen's heart was withering. She was dying from a lack of love.

That's why the relationship with Susan was so compelling for her. Here was a woman who was sweet and strong, needful of Karen's love and yet seemingly equipped to love and even to take care of her in certain ways. She saw in Susan a lost part of herself. Cut off from her own heart, Karen was cut off from her real needs. Like Jim, she needed to make peace with herself. She needed to befriend and learn to love the vulnerable, receptive little girl within.

But Karen's gender crisis was also, in a sense, the reverse of Jim's. Like most men struggling homosexually, Jim needed a boost of healthy masculine power in order to rise out of the feminine. He was stagnating in his immaturities. He needed to align with his masculinity. Only then could he begin to press through his fearful resistances to whole heterosexual relating. On the other hand, Karen needed to realign with the true feminine. She knew strength, but that strength had become a defense against the profound fears and vulnerabilities within. She needed to re-experience the rhythms of her heart.

Karen's heart craved tenderness. Given that love, she could begin to sort out what were real strengths and what were defenses against her anxious inner realities. Only the transforming power of true love could start to set aright the imbalance in her gender identity. (For more information on the healing of gender identity, please see *Pursuing Sexual Wholeness* guidebook, chapter 12.)

The Process of Sexual Development

As we've seen, clarity and security in a child's gender identity seem to have a significant impact on that child's sexual development. A major study conducted in 1981 cites one significant, recurring theme among the hundreds of homosexual adults who were interviewed: a recollection of being ''different'' from one's own gender peer group in childhood.[1] The study gives no reasons for this difference; that wasn't its intent. My personal and ministry experience leads me to conclude that a number of factors converge upon the young boy or girl in such a way that dispose him or her to detaching from the goodness of personal gender identity. The boy at odds with his ''boyness,'' the girl at odds with her ''girlness,'' are vulnerable to an intensifying identity crisis that will express itself in homoerotic feelings prior to or during early adolescence.

Clearly, this point of view emphasizes a progressive, developmental approach to sexuality—unlike some who view human beings as locked into their sexual orientation at birth or in the first five years of life. I view sexual identity as a bit more fluid and subject to variables that begin in the womb but don't cease to affect one's sexual development until early adulthood. I also have a difficult time accepting any *one* reason as *the* cause of homosexuality.

This applies to those who believe that homosexuality is inborn. That conclusion is simply too great a leap of faith given the lack of solid evidence to support it. However, current research seems to suggest certain hormones affect how we feel about ourselves as male and female. We may be born with a disposition to certain attitudes and aptitudes that are unique to being either male or female. But the research has yet to determine that those who grow up to be homosexually inclined do so because of imbalances in these particular hormones.

It's enough to say at this point that how we feel about our gender identities is crucial to sexual development. So I'll concentrate on what appear to be the greater influences that encounter us outside the womb as we emerge into adulthood.

To begin with, let me set down a theological understanding of sexual development and its breakdown. (For more information on a developmental view of sexuality, please see *Pursuing Sexual Wholeness* guidebook, chapter 6.) The Genesis account helps us to understand that the goal of adult sexuality is the capacity for whole, heterosexual relating. Wholeness may be defined in several ways—a sufficiently secure sense of one's own maleness and femaleness that liberates a desire for the other, the capacity to commit to another, the ability to engage sexually in the context of merging soul, spirit *and* body with another.

I want to elaborate here on the first point—having a sufficiently secure sense of one's gender to relate heterosexually. Jim and Karen didn't realize that security during their formative years. Spiritually speaking, that insecurity ravaged them. It rendered both naked and ashamed in their self-worth and sexual identities. Both hobbled into adolescence and early adulthood. Anxiety and uncertainty marked almost every attempt at fitting in, at finding love and purpose. Unlike most, for whom gender security is a given, Jim and Karen experienced gender as a kind of phantom that haunted them. Fear led to rebellion against their bodies and against those who incited their fears. Instead of growing into an increasingly clear and powerful sense of their identities as men and women, Jim and Karen felt stunted.

That breakdown in gender development breaks God's heart because He wants His sons and daughters to be whole, to be able to grow up into the fullness of His will. For our purposes here, that means the freedom to grow out of gender insecurity and the same-sex fixation that can result from it. It means the freedom to move into whole heterosexuality and the capacity to relate to members of the same sex as friends, not objects of erotic desire.

It also breaks God's heart that the fallen, deceived world in which His children live can render a person tragically vulnerable to gender brokenness and provide false ways to fix it, such as through homosexuality. Satan clearly has a great deal invested in this breakdown. If he can keep boys or girls alienated from the beauty and power of their gender, he has scored a major victory for the kingdom of darkness.

The shadow of fear and rebellion shrouds those children. It belittles them and distorts their original innocence. Anyone who has witnessed a man or woman being conformed to the image of the gay life-style and mind-set can discern a spiritual

121

disfigurement. The awesome reality of gender is contorted by the years of deception, of straining to glimpse some kind of wholeness in the broken reflection of same-sex lovers.

Instead of rounding out and illuminating one's true gender identity, each homosexual encounter constrains the true self. The young woman grows old and gray too quickly, with an outer toughness that shields her heart. The young man pursues his illusions until they entrap him, rendering him an old man still grasping after some cheap fix of masculinity. That's the enemy's domain. And God, in His infinite compassion, provides the way of deliverance. His heart may be broken by the brokenness of His children, but His love provides the power to restore them to their true identity.

Reordering Gender Identity

Jesus is the deliverer. He is the true image of God who receives anyone who recognizes the brokenness of his own image. Through His Holy Spirit, He begins to set aright the awesome gender realities that have become distorted.

Jesus is uniquely equipped to do this work because His life and ministry revealed the profound nature of gender wholeness. He operated out of the anointed rhythm of the feminine and the masculine. Before He acted, He listened; He was alive to the real feminine, the capacity to receive from the Father. That responsive quality was fundamental to His obedience. For how could Jesus obey unless His heart was yielded to the initiative of His Father?

Having received His Father's will, Jesus moved. He was powerful and purposeful in carrying out that will, empowered by the creative, life-changing strength of the Creator. In that regard, Jesus embodied masculinity at its best. His maleness resonated with incredible power and authority tempered by submission to the Father. His authority was thus redemptive, working in us the gender wholeness that enables us to live out the Father's will for our sexuality.

Let me again use the examples of Karen and Jim to clarify this reordering of gender identity. Jim's crisis, as we've seen, involved a detachment from the masculine. He consciously distanced himself from what he perceived to be an aggressive, cruel and rejecting approach to life and failed to see his need for a powerful center, an inner core of strength out of which he could approach life with gusto, not timidity.

Jesus' entry into his life united Jim with this true yearning of his heart. Jesus began by affirming Jim and breaking down some of the false images of masculinity under which he was laboring. Through the renewing of the Holy Spirit and affirming relationships with Christian men, Jim received the truth that the real masculine involves empowering love, not arbitrary, unbridled expressions of power. He listened to and believed words of love from his heavenly Father. The Lord united Jim's soul with a lifeline of care that was distinctly masculine.

For the first time, he realized that a sense of power and real confidence could be awakened in oneself *through relationships*. Women had always been the vessels of love for him. Now, through the Lord and solid Christian brothers, Jim discovered that others could build him up in a love that was distinctly masculine.

Over time, the power of love became a dynamic reality in Jim's life. He began not only to receive that power from others, but also to own that power as his own. His was not a prideful and soulish claim; it was one bestowed upon him by the Father through Jesus. The Spirit of Jesus now resides in Jim, awakening him to his inheritance as a son. And God has given Jim a heart for the unsaved. Instead of the illusory realm of homosexuality, he now lives according to the true realities of the kingdom of light. He enjoys nothing better than helping others enter into the light.

This transition from gender alienation to the radical empowering of Jim's masculinity hasn't always been easy. Jesus never claimed that true discipleship would be. But, as Jim continues to operate out of the empowering of the Holy Spirit, he is transformed, moment by moment. Jesus enables him to stand as an effectual man of God.

Karen made friends with the feminine through *her* relationship with Jesus. This also took time. As we've already seen, much of Karen's early Christian life was spent performing good Christian deeds. It wasn't until her performance fell apart that she faced her profound need for love. And God revealed Himself to her with tenderness and mercy, upholding her throughout the painful separation from Susan. She began to recognize that she didn't have to *do* anything to be loved by God. She simply needed to sit at His feet and receive His care.

Now that was disorienting! Karen had operated so long in the broken masculine—thinking and doing the right things—that she felt helpless and frightened at the prospect of learning *simply to be* before the Lord.

Gradually, with the cooperation of wise prayer counselors, the Holy Spirit reunited Karen with her heart's need for the nurture and rest of the Lord. Jesus revealed Himself to her in words and pictures that opened up a whole new dimension of the Christian life. She began to trust Him with the deep affairs of her heart. For the first time, Karen relied on Jesus as the Lord of her life. She ceased striving to attain His acceptance and submitted to His loving presence.

Unbeknownst to Karen, the Lord was restoring her femininity through her renewed trust in Him. But that healing required something more. She needed to be reconciled to the feminine as expressed in the Christian women around her. Her fears were not unwarranted. She understood that many women live in slavish devotion to men. Instead of becoming whole themselves, they immaturely grasp after wholeness in romance and marriage. Karen needed the assurance that the true feminine wasn't synonymous with submission to broken heterosexuality. She had experienced that deception in her own family.

To break through that fear, Jesus provided her with some good Christian role models, women who loved Jesus and relied on Him in their careers, their various ministries, and their pursuit of heterosexual intimacy. Karen was grateful to discover that a woman could be submitted to Jesus and not to heterosexual abuse. At the same time, she discovered a softness and vulnerability in these women, qualities that attracted her. They were alive to their need for the masculine in the Lord and in men. Yet they weren't crippled without a man because of the Lord's strength in them, His masculine arm that enabled them to stand as whole women in their own right.

Karen discovered that the true feminine facilitates real strength. Submission to Jesus resulted in His empowering her with the authority of the Holy Spirit. Like Jim, she learned to listen and receive the affirming words of the Father. She discovered the unique way in which her Father upholds her as a daughter. Protective and empowering, He frees Karen to praise Him for the unique beauty and vulnerability that are hers as a woman.

EIGHT

Making Peace With Our Parents

Much of my early sexual development was marked by alienation from my own masculinity. I felt inadequate and ill-suited for maleness. A lot of that stemmed from emotional detachment from my father, a move fostered as much by my own expectations and misperceptions as it was by his deficiencies. That dissociation was strengthened by cyclical rejection from male peers, beginning in grade school and continuing throughout adolescence. Distanced from my father and my male peers, I developed strong homosexual yearnings. I didn't realize the hurt and judgment I held toward the male population. I also didn't realize the degree to which

I was at odds with my own masculinity.

Then I became a Christian, and God began doing an incredible work of reconnecting me with my true identity. And as in Jim's and Karen's cases, the Holy Spirit started to restore my gender identity apart from my conscious realization of that process. God was empowering and aligning me with genuine masculinity. But deeper resistances remained, in particular the defensive separation from Dad and men in general. Although controlled, homosexual lust continued to be fueled by my inability to connect truly with other men. I was also beginning to struggle with pornography.

Finally, I submitted my soul to some exploration. What was going on that kept the homosexual feelings alive? I discovered the unnatural lack of feeling I had toward my father. At closer glance, I became aware of deep feelings of anger and resentment toward him that I had suppressed for years. Once these feelings surfaced and the source of hurt was identified, I could release him from my judgments. That broadened to include the male peers who had rejected me.

I honestly felt naked, very raw. My soul was exposed. But that also gave the Lord the opportunity to change my soul from its old way of coping with hurt. I began to weep at how deep was my need for male friendship. Something in my soul cried out for companionship that was affirming and affectionate but nonbinding. I didn't want sex or romance from men—I wanted buddies! I had experienced years of deprivation from positive sources of male affirmation, and my soul was further abused by my efforts to feed that deprivation homoerotically. God reduced me to that deeper level of healing in order to separate the true from the false.

Once the defensive alienation was released, I could admit my need for whole, same-sex relationships. I could then surrender the false ways of meeting that need through pornography or romanticizing friendships.

As that part of my story illustrates, an essential part of the healing process is coming to terms with the role our parents played in our gender development. No child is *born* with a sure confidence in his gender and in his capacity to love and be loved. That identity develops through interaction with others. And the most significant "others" are our parents. They're the first and most influential example of what male and female are and what heterosexual love is all about. Further, they're the lifeline that enables children *to become* good examples to *their* children.

Understanding the subtleties of the parent-child relationship is critical. What one child in a family may freely receive from a parent, a sibling may not. A breach of parental trust in the eyes of one child may be an accepted, standardized form of behavior in the eyes of another. The former may shut out the accused parent, while the latter may hunger for more of what the parent can give. In other words, we must recognize the parent-child relationship is extremely complex.

That's why one child in a family may develop homosexual vulnerabilities while his brother, exposed to some of the same parental influences, may not. He has a different mechanism with which he processes the influences. For example, he may remain more open to their father than his brother. Instead of detaching from him, he's able to use their father's influence to help secure his masculine identity.

But these variables don't diminish the importance of the relationship that parents either do or don't nurture with their children. Every child, regardless of personality, needs the covering and protection of his parents. Parental love builds the child's sense of worth. Neglect crushes it.

Parents function like scaffolding around a slow-growing skyscraper. They provide structure that encompasses the child and lends form and meaning to the life emerging within. As the child grows, the covering changes; the parents' proximity and intensity of interaction shift with each new stage of development. But big gaps in that scaffolding—in the covering God intends to protect and shape the child—will mean vulnerabilities in whatever area the child is uncovered. And the result can be a breakdown in the emergence of a child's whole and secure personal identity.

For our purposes, I want to focus on the gaps in parental covering that can lead to a child's gender insecurity. I've described in detail some of the factors in Karen's and Jim's family histories that contributed to their gender identity crises. For both of them, exploring these relationships was very difficult. Both had a lot invested in protecting their families from any hint of dysfunction. But as they realized that much hurt and anger remained in their hearts toward their parents, they also understood that denial was no longer a blissful option.

Obedience to Jesus—to His call for outward displays of love to match the heart's purity (the theme of the Sermon on the Mount)—compelled Karen and Jim to deal with the very real breakdown both had experienced in parental relationships. They saw that the breakdown continued to render them unwhole in their sexual and gender identities. And the Lord taught them that the desire to be reconciled to their parents could only be realized if they began to name and release to Him the sins and wounds that had marked those relationships.

So it is with each of us. God wants us to love our parents wholly, in truth. Facing what actually happened in the course of one's development is a crucial first step. It enables forgiveness to be applied at the level for which it's intended; it frees us to move beyond the point of deprivation and wounding toward a goal of growth and reconciliation.

Parental Roles in Shaping Gender Identity

Both parents are critical to the securing of a child's gender identity. But their roles are different. The same-sex parent provides the main source of gender identification. Mom represents to her daughter what femaleness is all about. Dad conveys to his son the main symbols and attributes of maleness. Whether whole or not, these expressions of gender continue to be the primary influence on the child's development.

As mentioned before, parents do more than exhibit certain behaviors and attitudes; they also provide the conduit through which the child receives (or resists) his inheritance. That conduit is the relationship itself. So the influence of the same-sex parent isn't based solely on his or her personal wholeness. It must also be assessed according to interpersonal wholeness—the degree to which the parent actually bonded with the child and through intimate relationship with him awakened and nourished his gender identity.

A study conducted by George Rekers supports the vital role of the relationship itself. He found that the degree of closeness between same-sex parent and child was more critical to the child's secure gender identity than were the actual gender attributes modeled by the parent.[1]

Thus, a whole, affirming relationship between a child and the same-sex parent undercuts the potential for homosexual development, while a broken relationship may have the opposite effect. Elizabeth Moberly, a research psychologist, has written several key works that explore how powerful the connection is between the same-sex parent and child, especially in the early years of bonding and attachment. Her books—*Psychogenesis*, *Homosexuality: A New Christian Ethic* and *The Psychology of Self and Other*—persuasively convey the reality that in each boy or girl lies an emerging sense of his maleness or her femaleness that must be blessed and called forth by a whole relationship with the same-sex parent. Author Gordon Dalbey reiterates this truth in his powerful book *Healing the Masculine Soul*.

Dr. Moberly pays special attention to the results of a break-down in that connection. She cites many factors that can cause a rupture in the relationship, such as parental abuse, emotional and physical absence, death, illness, neglect, parents' per-sonal problems, and so on.[2] That break can block the child's capacity for same-sex intimacy and identification, which in turn obstructs secure gender development.

Given the various factors on the parents' end that can cause a breakdown in relationship, Dr. Moberly highlights the child's reaction to the parents. She refers to a protective mechanism she calls "defensive detachment." Here the child responds to what is perceived as painful and untrustworthy in the parent by detaching emotionally. As seen in my story at the beginning of this chapter, a kind of invisible wall is erected that protects the child from further hurt.

Behind the defensive detachment, the child's tremendous need for same-sex intimacy and identification remains. But the need stews in an emotional pressure cooker. On the one hand is the yearning. But on the other hand, the breakdown in relationship with the same-sex parent and the walls of distrust and disdain that protect the child keep the need con-tained. The need ends up being stuffed down into the child's soul.

That defensive detachment pollutes the child's response to his own gender. Not only does he distrust the parent, but he also comes to distrust his own adequacy as a gender person and to reject himself. The wall of detachment thickens and blocks out a lot more than just parental wounding; it resists even healthy and appropriate same-sex offerings. Positive aspects of masculinity and femininity are rejected due to their association with the troubled parental relationship. For example, masculine strength is written off as abusive, feminine vulnerability as weak and helpless. The child grows timid and defensive with same-sex peers, preferring isolation to healthy engagement.

Fear and insecurity mark the child's perception of his own sex. With gender more a point of conflict than of hearty resolve, the child totters into adolescence off-center, vulnerable to false ways of handling the crisis.

Dr. Moberly's research shows that when the nonerotic need for intimacy and identification with the same sex is walled off for a number of years behind the defensive detachment, the need assumes a heightened intensity and urgency. When fueled with the fire of adolescent sexuality, it becomes inflamed by erotic intent. The individual knows nothing about this, but the homosexual tendencies he faces are really red-flag warnings that deeper, nonerotic needs are surfacing from the soul.

When strugglers understand there's a normal and legitimate need at the core of their sexual tendencies, they find the truth liberating. They aren't perverts who love evil for evil's sake. An innocent, involuntary need is expressing itself in a broken way. That grants them the profound freedom to care for their needs while not submitting them to a false solution.

Partners are needed, but not those who will fuel the falsehood that at the core one is homosexual. Strugglers need God, the Holy Other, to inform the fluctuations of the soul. They also need those who can uphold them as whole persons while helping to meet the underlying emotional craving for same-sex intimacy and identification.

The Opposite-Sex Parent

Detachment from the same-sex parent, from same-sex peers, and ultimately from one's own gender wholeness is the primary root of homosexuality. But other factors help shape homosexual development as well.

The opposite-sex parent, for instance, plays an important role in affirming a child's gender, but in a way that differs from that of the same-sex parent. Through the affirmation and love of the opposite-sex parent, the child acquires a sense of worth and ability to relate well to the opposite sex.

These good things happen if the opposite-sex parent continues to be a parent and upholds the child as a child. That is, the parent doesn't try to be a peer or merely a good friend to the child but maintains the boundary of his adult status relative to the child. The parent's adult needs for intimacy and worth are submitted to other adults. Children are not looked to as the parent's lifeline to wholeness.

Furthermore, the young girl's or boy's development into adulthood must be affirmed without a hint of seductive intent. Any indication that the opposite-sex parent is aroused by the child's sexual maturation can break the sanctified boundary intended to protect the young. An incestuous gaze or touch can cast a shadow on the child's capacity to view opposite-sex peers clearly. Instead of seeing the normal and appropriate desire of a young girlfriend or boyfriend for what it is, the victimized child sees the broken image of a lustful parent looming over each innocent encounter.

Another key factor is the kind of marriage that was modeled to the child. Did the parents live out a pattern of heterosexual love that a child would want to follow? Or was the marital relationship riddled with unresolved conflict, continual breakdowns in communication, and, finally, the spouses' detachment from one another expressed in a cool coexistence or divorce? If the marriage was in some ways abusive, who appeared to be the abuser? The victim?

A child can reject completely the prospect of marriage given exposure to long-term abusive marital patterns. That effect is heightened if one parent sides the child with himself against the other. The child enters into adulthood prematurely; the boundary protecting him from adult conflict is broken. He is "force-fed" an often skewed perception of the one parent's "evil" and the "good" parent's innocence. For many young people, unaffirmed in their genders and confused by a broken relationship with one or both parents, a damaged perception of marriage may be the final push into the uncharted realm of homosexuality. (For added information on the critical role of the family in sexual development, read chapter 7 of the *Pursuing Sexual Wholeness* guidebook.)

Time and again, I've witnessed strugglers coming up against a barrier to heterosexual relating caused by a perception that the opposite-sex parent abused his spouse. One counselee had a profound mistrust of women due to his mother's controlling, verbally abusive interaction with her rather passive husband. Karen's history involving an unfaithful father led her to distrust men, an attitude accentuated by her mother's confiding in Karen all her pain. But obviously, as Karen's case reveals, the seeming "victim" in the marriage may also become the impetus for the child's shutting down. Karen detached from her femininity because she equated it with her mother's *inability to rise above her victim status*. The male counselee mentioned above resented his father for not being man enough to stop his dominating wife.

Other Dangers

While interaction with parents is key to the formation of gender and sexual identity, other factors can also break down healthy development. But even here the destructive effect of these factors will depend in part on the health of the parent-child relationship. Trauma inflicted outside the family will be less devastating if the child can seek healing and support within the family. Sexual abuse is one such trauma.

Many homosexual strugglers in Desert Stream are dealing with the effects of sexual abuse. The abuse itself is not the cause of homosexual tendencies. But if family dysfunction has left the child vulnerable, abuse outside the home can inflict tremendous damage on his sense of gender security and sexual wholeness.

The child's thin, developing boundaries of self cave in under the weight of an adult's sexual perversion. These boundaries are intended to lend structure and protection to the child's sense of self. The sexual abuser defies both. In a moment, the child is initiated into the realm of adult sexuality, an experience intended only for committed, consenting partners. He can't contain the foreign experience; he's not intended to. The abuser leaves the victim disoriented by shame, a profound sense of dirtiness and the crippling anxiety that life is no longer safe, that one has little control over what another may arbitrarily foist upon him.

The effects on sexual identity are different for men and women. For the young girl who is already unaffirmed and detached from her femininity, sexual abuse seals her distrust of men and of the goodness of her female sexuality. The abuser becomes a symbol of maleness—harsh, controlling, an overpowering figure driven by his genitals. The abuse further reinforces her misconception that females are victims and males are victimizers. The arms of another woman connote safety and security. In contrast to the broken image of heterosexuality seared upon her by the abuse, a female lover beckons like an oasis.

Male sexual abuse is usually homosexual in nature. For all boys, such experiences are shameful and degrading. But for boys already cut off from and yet craving masculine care, erotic encounters with an adult male may afford them a twisted kind of affirmation.

If the abuse is consistent and paired with a kind of tenderness, the child may come to equate eroticism with genuine care. Perhaps the only male who initiates a relationship with him is the abuser! This in no way discounts the degradation involved in the abuse. But the child desperate for the masculine may feed off even diseased versions of it. His deprivations dispose him to sorely misinterpreting the abuser's evil. Love and homoeroticism converge, and that distortion may fuel homosexual pursuits later in life. (For more information on the effects of sexual abuse for both male and female strugglers, please see appendix 3 in *Pursuing Sexual Wholeness* guidebook, and write Desert Stream Ministries about ordering the author's unpublished article "The Inner Healing of Homosexual Abuse Victims.")

When broken relationships have caused a person to set up defenses against the perceived agent of hurt and abuse, what does the struggler do with those walls? How is one freed to love others nondefensively? That's especially relevant with parents. For in order to become whole and free in one's gender identity, one must make peace with them. Mom and Dad are the human lifeline; through them sons and daughters receive much of their inheritance as people, gender and otherwise. To be cut off from them is to be cut off from oneself. Some of that inheritance hurts; it has broken or stunted the young life. But some of it empowers and unites the child with his true, unique personality.

Accordingly, the struggler must face the truth about his relationship with his parents in order to progress to sexual wholeness. Reconciling with them (and others of significant influence) liberates the capacity to love.

Reconciling With Parents

The first and most obvious step in reconciling with parents is naming the wound, the points of division that caused the struggler to detach from them. In other words, he must first identify what's been broken.

For some, this can be the hardest step of all. Many of us have adopted the insidious habit of denying how others have wounded us, especially parents. In an effort to protect them, as well as ourselves, we whitewash the feelings of anger, resentment and hurt that are rooted in their sins. We may operate under the theory, ''They did the best they could.'' And that's probably true. Many wounds inflicted by parents were not deliberate. The wounds may relate to a prolonged period of emotional neglect, a lack of affirmation and acceptance, the effects of a broken marriage and so on. But no amount of rationalization can heal the inner wounds that continue to flare up and cause a person to wall off as he interacts with his parents in the present.

Behind that shield, the homosexual struggler has remained an angry, wounded, needy child, unable to grow beyond the point of hurt and captive to his own means of defending himself. His gender development remains bound up in childhood fears, rejections and disappointments that prompted him to wall off in the first place. And now he's overwhelmed with homosexual desire. But his craving can never be satisfied until he faces its source—his detachment from those who conceived him.

The struggler must address that crucial mistrust and detachment from the same-sex parent and, secondarily, from the parent of the opposite sex. Only then can the legitimate need for emotional connection with one's own sex be distinguished from lust. Only then can he truly receive from God and others the genuine sources of intimacy and identification needed to become a whole member of his own sex. As the defensive detachment is identified, hurts are surfaced, and forgiveness is applied to the source of detachment. The struggler is freed to embrace the wonderful desire to become a whole man. With that reality intact, homoeroticism can be laid down as the lie it is.

The Need to Forgive

Forgiveness is central to breaking through that defensive detachment. Having identified the person(s) from whom he's detached and the precise nature of the hurt, the struggler then possesses the raw material needed to release the offender.

But before actually going to the cross with the burdens at hand, the struggler may need the time and space to acknowledge and resolve the emotional pain that accompanies defensive detachment. Much of the pain has been stuffed—that's why he detached from the parent or peer in the first place, because he didn't want to feel the pain anymore! He needs to talk to God about the hurt or anger that seeps up from the soul. Talking with a trusted friend, writing feelings down furiously in a journal, beating a pillow—any of these can help to release the pent-up pain that results from not getting what was wanted or needed from a parent.

Sometimes a struggler just has to grieve for the loss of love and affirmation that can never be recaptured. Maybe it's a matter of grieving for the damage caused by another's violation of personal boundaries through physical or sexual abuse or inappropriate emotional bonding. Before the source of wounding can be brought honestly into the light of God's grace and forgiveness, the struggler may need to allow the emotional implications of the offense to catch up with him, to face him openly. That enables the burden of another's sin to take on its appropriate weight. Then placing that burden on the shoulders of Christ will afford the soul a more profound and sobering release.

Accordingly, the next step in undoing defensive detachment involves applying the grace of Jesus to the offense and the offender. In the same way we are freed from personal sin by agreeing with the sufficiency of Christ's crucifixion and resurrection on our behalf, so we are freed from *interpersonal* sin by applying the ministry of the cross to those who have sinned against us (see Matt. 18:23-33). As Jesus has forgiven us our sins, so we forgive those who have wounded us (see Matt. 6:12). We release our right to stand as that person's judge, yielding control of the burden of vengeance and retribution to Jesus. The cross becomes the resting place for the burden of unforgiveness.

What a release! We were not created to bear the burden of another's sin toward us; the resulting anger, resentment and bitterness can actually destroy the body and soul. In the case of the homosexual struggler, unforgiveness can constrain his already unaffirmed gender identity.

Through our willingness to forgive, however, Jesus replaces the power of defensive detachment with the authority of His cross. As the sin of another is released to Him, Jesus mediates in us a fresh wave of grace and objectivity toward the offender. Pain and anger become subordinated by the greater reality of Jesus' mercy. The cross—not the offense—becomes the symbol that governs our response to the object of detachment. The child within that was previously walled off becomes rooted in Jesus' sufficiency for the wounder. That child is freed to rise out of his constrained position and to accept the parent or peer in light of who he was and who he is now.

Through forgiveness, we come to see in the offender another adult whose assets are matched only by his warts. We see ourselves. And as Christ's grace has been sufficient for us, we entrust the one who hurt us to the sufficiency of His grace. (This essential forgiveness process is described in much greater detail in *Pursuing Sexual Wholeness* guidebook, chapter 11 and appendix 5.)

Does that mean that we and Dad or Mom, or we and the person who abused us, will become best buddies? Not at all. It simply means that we're now freed to love the person without being constrained by the defensive detachment. In some relationships we'll need to establish new boundaries.

For example, Jim walked through the process of forgiving both his mother and father. As was described in chapter 7, Jim's father was emotionally distant and critical. As was not mentioned, his mother tended to view Jim as "her special child," and she continues to treat him as a rather genderless confidante. Thus, Jim faced two completely different rhythms in his parental relationships—a father from whom he had detached and continued to distance himself, and a mother with whom he was too close, a relationship that cast a shadow on his desire to walk as a strong and whole man.

Jim's forgiving his parents for their brokenness toward him resulted in establishing two different sets of boundaries. He felt freed to initiate more in relationship to his father. He had no illusions about intense intimacy, but he genuinely desired to love him more heartily. With his mother, he needed to pull back and establish a boundary that was appropriate to being an adult male. That was hard for Jim at first; he didn't want to hurt her. But he couldn't return to the chatty, somewhat effeminate role he had always played with her. He needed "to cut the apron strings" by standing upright in relationship with her and loving her as a son *who was also a man*. Jim is still in the process of figuring out what that means. But Jesus is sufficient to empower him to establish these new boundaries.

Karen faced a similar pattern in relationship to her parents, although she was forgiving *two* people from whom she had detached. Her mother was the hardest one for her to forgive; she felt protective of her, almost maternal in her insisting that "poor, victimized Mom" was without sin. But God was faithful to reveal the real thoughts and intents of Karen's heart. Beneath the role of protecting mother, she hated her mom's impotence in the face of her father's abuse and adultery. Karen needed to pull back and wrestle with the hard truth that she wasn't given the freedom to be a child by her mother, and that her mother's brokenness crippled her capacity to embrace her own femaleness as a good gift. That took time to identify and forgive. In the end, it granted her a much truer compassion for her mother.

Reconciling with her father was terribly difficult as well. She felt rage toward him, and to some extent, she still feels a lot of anger. But she has willed to release him to Jesus. And she's taking steps to get to know him for who he is now, not who *he was* according to her mother's running commentary on his abusiveness.

Freedom to Embrace

One of the most exciting outcomes of the power of forgiveness, especially as applied to defensive detachment toward the same-sex parent, is the freedom it grants the struggler to embrace the wonderful attributes of that parent. Defensive detachment may protect one from another's deficits, but it also prevents one from embracing his good.

Both Karen and Jim began to see that her mother and his

father had a lot of excellent qualities to which they were heirs. Jim's eyes were opened to his dad's savvy and resourcefulness in mechanics, and he sought out his help in mechanical matters like car troubles and minor carpentry tasks. Karen saw that, in spite of her mother's ''victim'' mentality and lack of healthy boundaries, she had tried to be a devoted parent. Karen saw a genuinely unselfish woman who in many ways placed her kids' needs above her own. That quality gave her new respect for her mother. Perhaps one day Karen will emulate that quality in her own family.

I, too, have been freed to embrace the many good qualities of my father and to give grace to us both in our mutual weaknesses. He is worthy of my respect. Apart from Jesus, he is the closest human reflection of my own masculinity. I praise Jesus for making a way for me to return to my father. The past is past; Jesus has died with my defensive detachment from my father. Now Jesus lives as the catalyst of our relationship. I want to love my father as Jesus has loved me. And I want to receive from him every great and empowering aspect of my inheritance as his son.

Making peace with my father has also helped me to make peace with my masculinity. I praise God for what in me is strong and true; I seek Him for what remains to be empowered and matured. I've made peace, too, with my ongoing need for whole relationships with other men. Gratefully, that need has been purged of any lustful intention. And my wholeness as a heterosexual man frees me to affirm my own children. God has given me the authority to call forth in them the real goodness of their worth as people—specifically, as people graced with gender. He's also given me compassion for their vulnerabilities and failures as children in the same way that He has compassion on my failures as a parent.

NINE

The Flight
Into Addiction

A s you read in chapter 1, my homosexual tendencies developed through my early years and became highly eroticized at age twelve. After my first homosexual experience at age sixteen, I quickly developed an addiction to it because of the affirmation and sense of acceptance I was finally receiving from other men. My flight into addiction was all too typical. Between the early breakdowns in strugglers' relationships and gender identities and the application of forgiveness so that healing can begin, they develop patterns of living that are addictive and destructive. They learn to compromise their bodies and souls in desperate attempts at finding love.

Here's another way of looking at it. Those who struggle homosexually don't often possess a normal, healthy set of boundaries that protect the soul and mediate a necessary give and take of love and affirmation. We've seen how critical a child's early relationships are in the development of those boundaries. Unaffirmed and unprotected, strugglers submit themselves to broken ways of getting their needs met.

That brokenness may express itself in chaotic relationships or anonymous sexual encounters. Both expressions are addictive, consuming and difficult to break off even in the face of a loving, powerful God and the deep healing He affords. That healing frees them to begin to obey the Father's call to purity and maturity in their relationships.

But walking out that obedience, especially when they've been addicted for a long time, is a hard task in its own right. Yet walk they must. Strugglers must get free in order to move into whole and life-affirming relationships. Broken patterns of relating must be faced and forsaken, and real needs must be identified. That frees them to approach the meeting of those needs from a whole and sanctified vantage point. In turn they're freed to love out of the pervasive love of Jesus.

The Nature of Addiction

When I talk about sexual and emotional addiction, I'm referring to a persistent (or at least a habitual) preoccupation with a sexual fantasy, behavior or person with whom one is infatuated. The focus on any of these sparks a sexual arousal, and in most cases a period of toying with the object of desire that will result eventually in orgasm. An addict will feel controlled by the object of desire, will spend inordinate amounts of time pursuing the object, and can identify the central role the object of desire plays in his life. Much as he may feel out of control and depressed by it, he may remain committed to the source of addiction.

The power of God's love must be our primary impetus and motivator as we seek to escape addiction. He frees us to desire the greater good. The Lord hates addiction, because He hates watching His children become conformed to evil. Instead He wants us to be conformed to His will (see Rom. 12:1-2).

Many have wrestled vainly against addiction because of some vague sense of God's disdain. Weakly, detached from His love and power, they try to break free from the chains of addiction to earn His love and power. That doesn't work; we need His advocacy in order to be free. As Paul wrote in Romans 12:21, "Do not be overcome by evil, but overcome evil with good." God wants to liberate us from bondage *through His love*. And that powerful love is activated in us as we take hold of the inspired declaration of Paul, "I will not be mastered by anything" (1 Cor. 6:12).

God lives in us and cries out to guard our hearts and minds from illusions that pollute our purity and cripple our hope for greater wholeness. Only by heeding His voice and taking hold of His love can we be motivated aright and know the pleasure of pure hearts and minds mastered only by Jesus.

Anyone who has ever wrestled with an addictive relationship or behavior pattern knows how much that "fix" conflicts with the pervasive love of Jesus. Addiction is fueled by a restless, consuming energy that compels us to cover ourselves with another person or set of images in defense against the light of Jesus. We become motivated by the inner void, the memory of sensual pleasure, the prospect of the unknown.

Racing toward the object of desire, we run harder in a futile effort to escape the fact that God is with us. Much as we deny Him, we cannot shake Him. He continues to run alongside us. So we drink a little more, laugh a little harder, and ultimately fail in our attempts at establishing an outpost that contains the false love and excludes Him. I praise God for His stubbornness in never allowing me to lie down peacefully with my idols. He remains constant as the nagging, goading presence who renders every plunge into addiction ultimately miserable. And when we've tasted of His peace, the dark restlessness of addiction is revealed as the degrading act of inhumanity that it is.

I do not use the word *inhumanity* lightly. As we've seen, God has established certain boundaries to shield our humanity from broken expressions of sexuality. But sexually addictive patterns break into the sacred space within our humanity that God has deemed holy ground.

In other words, whenever a person commits an erotic act outside marriage, be it in thought or in action, a boundary has been violated. The body, soul and spirit receive a jolt of erotic energy that is not intended for one who cannot conceive that pleasure in a committed heterosexual union.

If a person continues to feed off these images or relationships, the sanctified boundaries break down all the more, and the erotic assault on one's humanity intensifies. Broken boundaries permit all kinds of demonically inspired debris to enter in and pollute the body, soul and spirit with false eroticism.

Tragically, many become acclimated to the stream of pollutants. Their hearts become calloused to the assault of fantasy, of that pornographic image or this illegitimate relationship. They may become deadened to the darkness wrought in that inner sanctuary where God alone should dwell. Each false expression we befriend becomes an enemy of the Real— Christ Jesus—who longs to rebuild our broken boundaries from the inside out. But first He must sensitize us to the evil, addictive quality of illegitimate eroticism.

Perhaps the greatest block we face in this process is denial. We don't want to admit we even have a problem with false eroticism, let alone an ongoing one. This may be especially true for those who have been knit into the Christian community for some time. They may feel that their giftedness and longevity as Christians, even the extent of their wholeness, excludes them from having an addictive erotic problem—or at least bars them from admitting it to anyone.

That was certainly my temptation. I was a pastor, a director of a healing ministry for homosexual strugglers, a husband and a father when I came to grips with my pornography addiction (see chapter 5). Did my role not presume greater wholeness? Should I not presume likewise and reframe my problem as a "bad habit" that God and I could solve without anyone else's knowing?

But how could God become even a part of the solution unless I was willing to face the reality of the evil? This was a real key for me. If God was to be Lord and redeemer of my addiction, sin's reality had to be faced entirely.

That meant admitting first of all that my mind and heart were oppressed by eroticism, a reality that severed intimacy with real people, especially my wife. And second, I needed help! I had to forsake the illusion that my periodic, rather detached confession of sin to God alone was sufficient. I needed concrete, tangible agents of Jesus to stand with me, helping me face the problem at hand, as well as its solution.

Karen and Jim faced the same tendency toward denial. Jim's temptation involved pornography and anonymous sexual activity. In some ways, his dealing with it paralleled my own. Karen's struggle was more subtle in that her addiction was a hybrid of the emotional and the erotic—all wrapped up in a "special friend" who readily became the driving force in her life.

After breaking up with Susan, Karen faced much loneliness, as well as many healing opportunities. As has been described already, the Lord ministered to Karen through the direct presence of the Holy Spirit and the intervention of caring Christians. But Karen remained needy and still entertained notions of that special girlfriend who would enter her life and complete her. She grew weary of staying accountable regarding her feelings toward Susan.

When Karen met another woman to whom she felt attracted, she chose to deny her erotic impulses. Instead she presented to others a picture of a whole, balanced friendship. But she allowed the still-weak boundaries surrounding her soul and her sexuality to be encroached upon by the desired other. She was utterly vulnerable to forsaking all and becoming one with that woman.

It wasn't until Karen engaged in sexual relations with her friend that she realized her deception. That experience birthed in Karen a new and sober awareness of her need to stay alive to her addictive tendencies.

The Need for Human Help

But obviously, it's not enough to be aware of one's neediness. Strugglers need a place to go with their vulnerability. *That's where confession of one's sexually addictive tendencies to God and trusted others is essential.* Addiction creates a kind of moral blindness. Having conceded time and again to the false object of desire, the heart becomes deceitful, unwilling and almost unable to disengage from its own destructive cycles. That's when strugglers must cast themselves upon the care and "sight" of others. Sexual addicts must admit, "I can't really trust myself in this area."

For the Christian, that will mean more than simply releasing the struggle to God in the safety of one's prayer closet. For years, the addict has prayed alone to the Father, and for years, the addictive cycle has continued alongside Christian service and comrades who knew nothing about the struggle. In a recent Living Waters group, I asked how many of the forty participants confessed their struggles with sexual addiction to close Christian friends. About thirty-two of the forty confessed only to God, which usually resulted in yielding to the temptation at hand.

Don't get me wrong. I'm not downplaying the power of prayer. I'm simply illustrating the nature of addiction, which involves a flight from reality into deception and illusion. I have counseled many who claimed to have a seemingly devoted relationship to Jesus while falling into sexual sin continually. They walled off their "double lives" as if they were a nonreality, or perhaps a habit pattern kept alive by another person altogether. The human personality can go to great lengths to protect itself from its own darkness.

The only bridge that can connect the two parts of the struggler—pious Christian and detached addict—is confession to other people who mediate the reality of Christ's grace and truth. The struggler needs the witness of *a human being*. Only a human agent of Jesus can encounter him squarely, speaking the truth, mirroring the gravity of the addiction and verbalizing Christ's liberating forgiveness.

Then the addict is freed to lay down the burden of shame and guilt at the foot of the cross. The illusion of solitary reliance on Jesus has been shattered by the inbreaking of the presence of Jesus through a Christian brother or sister.

The nonaddict must understand that sexual addiction is a flight from real relationships with other people. The addict becomes hooked on the deception that the hidden relationship with pornographic images or illicit lovers (real or imagined) is a more reliable source of love and affirmation than nonerotic relationships. Love becomes equated with eroticism, affirmation with orgasm. The result is always a breach of true intimacy, but that breach will express itself differently depending on the type of addiction.

Jim's flight into sexual addiction had an intensely alienating effect. He sought refuge from the pressures of work and the challenges of the Christian life. The guilt and belittlement he experienced after a fall increased his sense of alienation and caused him to detach all the more from the prospect of real intimacy within the body of Christ.

Karen's addictive tendencies and their alienating effect were a bit different. After the relationship with Susan ended, Karen was tempted to rush into others. That was good for her in a way. Previously, she had been detached from her need for others. Susan opened her up to a volcano of need that didn't cease to erupt after the relationship ended. The problem lay in her equating real intimacy with an exclusive, romantic and eroticized form of love.

When appropriate boundaries were violated again by Karen in her second homosexual relationship, she swung back into detachment, afraid of needing another for fear of perverting that need. Her addictive tendencies thus destabilized her commitment to whole relationships. Where she had rushed headlong into a relationship before, denying the addictive elements that fueled her, she now swung back into the safety and sterility of isolation.

Thus, addictive tendencies alienated both Jim and Karen from others. The healing of the addiction necessitated turning toward others who could love them wholly, without erotic intent.

A pioneer in the area of sexual addiction, Patrick Carnes wrote in his excellent book *Out of the Shadows*: "Recovery from addiction is the reversal of the alienation that is integral to the addiction. Addicts must establish roots in a caring community. With that support, addicts can stay straight as they struggle with a perspective for their lives."[1] (For more information on sexual addiction, read chapter 15 of *Pursuing Sexual Wholeness* guidebook.)

Caring for the Addict

How can the community care effectively for the addict? As we've seen, hearing the confession of sin and brokenness, then speaking Christ's word of forgiveness is crucial. You may be the first person to encounter the addict with the reality of love and concern, the first agent of light to shine on the hidden, shameful aspects of one's "other life." But where do you go from there? How can you help the addict to rebuild the sanctified boundaries that will enable him to stand upright and intact?

A good starting point is to understand how the deep craving for same-sex intimacy often expresses itself in the struggler. There are two common forms of expression: narcissism and relational idolatry. The narcissist remains guarded but seeks another's stimulation and even adoration sexually. The idolater lunges heart-first into another's center, defying all boundaries in a vain effort to find completion. Both postures are extremely addictive; both require special understanding and insight if the addict is to be redeemed.

Narcissism is a wrongful kind of self-love, a type that expresses itself in a preoccupation with one's own image. The narcissist's energies are invested in that image—building up the body (or toning it down), buying the right clothes, posturing in a way that will elicit a favorable response from others. The outer image so painstakingly crafted serves as a lure that can entice others, reel them in, and cause them to worship.

153

Sex or another's emotional infatuation does not connect with the narcissist's heart. Both merely grant the narcissist a rather flat and safe level of affirmation. Such feedback from others is assessed on the basis of how it reflects on self, not by the degree to which the narcissist experiences a true connection with people. Others are needed only to trump up his self-worth by adoring the image.

A huge ego? Not really. The narcissist is actually so wounded within, so lacking in genuine self-acceptance, that he has walled off the heart and all its true yearnings. No exposed heart, no risk of rejection. A cool and detached image, that others either admire or pass by, affords one much less pain—but no real love. The narcissist relies almost entirely on a rather impermeable image that may elicit the superficial stroke of another's arousal.

Homosexual strugglers may be especially vulnerable to narcissism because they've been deprived of a real sense of worth and wholeness as gender persons. That deprivation, coupled with the high anxiety and shame that many strugglers associate with conveying *feelings* of love for a member of the same sex (especially in men), may provide all of the raw material necessary to create a strong narcissistic tendency.

This is especially relevant to the male struggler. His heart is split off from his body, and yet he can work out his feelings of inadequacy by investing in his body, developing into a kind of physical "superman" who draws out the "cannibal compulsion" in others. His heart remains blocked from receiving true and healing affirmation for his masculinity, while his body receives a fallen and even demonized adoration from men who are as broken as he is.

The narcissist readily becomes addicted to this flat, orgasmic cycle of affirmation. Jim's history exemplifies this.

He was afraid to love other men—scared of his own inadequacy, fearful of their rejection. Even in the gay community, Jim had a hard time connecting with men. That wasn't helped by the shame he felt about his sexuality. But he wasn't really seeking sex; he wanted a friend, a buddy, often a father. At the time, he didn't know this. All he knew was the lure and rush of homosexual activity, coupled with deep feelings of fear and guilt.

Jim's solution was the defense of narcissism. He distanced himself from his loneliness and self-hatred by investing in his physical image. Through seducing others, he captured a perverse form of affirmation while remaining completely in control. He was surprised at how close he could get to another physically while still feeling utterly alone. This disparity between the heart's cry and his protective image drove him to Jesus. Even the most "successful" narcissist can endure its emptiness for only so long. (For more information on narcissism, please see *Pursuing Sexual Wholeness* guidebook, chapter 8. Special thanks to Alexander Lowen for his excellent book *Narcissism: Denial of the True Self*.)

In relation to God and others, Jim needed more than to confess having illicit sex. He needed to confess the fear and inadequacy that compelled him to prop up the seductive image. Jim didn't trust others; he didn't believe that people, especially men, could connect meaningfully with him.

To be called out of that world, and out from under the false image at hand, Jim needed to be wooed by the power of love. He needed others who could call him out. And he needed to risk laying down the image and the seductive posture in order to receive the love of others.

People in Jim's life needed to help him deal honestly with the "symptom" of addictive narcissism while also addressing the alienation and fear that fueled the symptom. They could do so by upholding him in whatever deeper or riskier disclosure he made. His detachment from the risk of intimacy and subsequent retreat into narcissism needed to be pointed out gently and challenged. When things got rough, he preferred to secure a one-night stand or a pornographic video rather than risk being loved by a Christian brother or sister.

However, the challenge to the narcissist not to retreat into erotic illusion implies he has someplace else to go. That requires the real love of other Christians. And it necessitates that the love sparked by fellowship will inflame the struggler's heart with the presence of Jesus.

His presence is the reality that grants the narcissist a mooring point, a source of security and strength. Into the void where fear, inadequacy and profound anxiety have dwelled, Jesus longs to enter. And through the release of the Holy Spirit, He can, but not without purging the pain that lies at the center of many addicts. That pain remains stored up inside and even increases as one submits himself to addictive solutions. Jesus wants access there so He can establish the healing ministry of the cross. Where death encroaches upon the soul, Jesus longs to assume its weight and establish His resurrection.

Jim experienced Jesus at the center of his pain. The Lord revealed the deep crack within his heart that distanced him from his father and his own masculinity; He also gave him a glimpse of his mother's inordinate closeness to him. At a level more profound than reason, Jim grieved over the brokenness—his parents', his own. He actually entered into the profound loneliness and anxiety that had marked much of his early life. As the pain was released through deep sobs, he felt incredibly small and naked, like a helpless animal in a forest full of predators.

Jesus met him there. He surrounded him with strong arms

and gazed upon him, His eyes ablaze with powerful compassion. Jim had never experienced the Lord's love that completely; it was deeper than his pain. Then the image changed from an outer sense of the Lord's presence to an inner one. It was as if Jesus were standing within his soul. He was at once crucified and resurrected—empathic to the wounds in Jim's soul while pouring the sweetness and surety of His presence into the broken and cracked places. That flooding of Jesus into Jim's pain established a new level of freedom for him to avail himself of the healthy sources of love around him.

Relational Idolatry

Addiction also expresses itself in relational idolatry. By that I mean the tendency of some strugglers to attempt to ease their pain through inappropriate bonding with members of the same sex. *Inappropriate* needs to be underscored, because *healthy* same-sex friendships are critical to the struggler's wholeness. By "inappropriate," I refer to highly dependent relationships that become eroticized, or at least romanticized.

Unlike the narcissist, whose brokenness compels him to erect boundaries that hide the true self, the idolater attempts to find himself by merging with another. Boundaries are violated by both parties. Lacking an inner sense of strength and well-being, the idolater is inordinately bent toward another as his source of love and power. He feels whole as long as the relationship appears to be intact. Threatened by the loss of the other, the inner void aches more intently and can elicit feelings of suicide or violence. The idolater builds an altar to the lover, who may be better defined as an object of worship. The creature is served over the Creator and is granted an authority intended only for the divine. (For more information on relational idolatry, please see *Pursuing Sexual Wholeness* guidebook, chapter 9.)

Karen's relational history can be described as a wide turn from narcissism into idolatry. Essentially, she defended herself from her disdain for men and longing for women through a kind of Christian narcissism. In flight from intimacy with others, she invested all in an image of obedience and spiritual discipline that shielded her from fear. That image finally broke under the weight of her intense neediness. Like a river overflowing its embankment, Karen's desires rose up and broke chaotically upon Susan. Thick boundaries gave way, leaving no boundaries at all. Karen was primed for an idolatrous relationship. Her hunger for touch, for affirmation, for companionship, for being special all converged on one person who was endowed with the impossible task of becoming Karen's all-in-all.

The situation was intensified by Karen's history of sexual abuse. Her boundaries as a young girl had been violated by the fondlings of an older neighborhood boy and two dismal sexual encounters with teenage males that bordered on date rape. She really had no model of how to express sexual need in a whole way.

Karen had swung from bondage to bondage—fear of man, fear of needing women. And now, needs exposed, she became captive to the addictive and boundless realm of relational idolatry. Its deception lies in bypassing the Creator. The creature is elevated to an unnatural and illusory position that he can never live up to. Lovers may ultimately reveal their "clay feet," but the addictive nature of idolatry feeds a consuming quest for completion through the creature, one relationship after another.

Karen had a hard time admitting her tendency toward idolatry. She resisted that confession on the basis of the good she experienced in each relationship. With both Susan and the following lover, she received a kind of care and attention that soothed the deep ache within. Her experience registered something closer to ecstasy than the agony befitting idol worship. These two relationships satisfied her need in a way that immediately made her defensive toward slapping the ''sin'' label on them and returning to a life of emotional sterility. The Christian narcissist had fallen. And she resisted repentance on the grounds that the falsehood of lesbianism was no worse than the false image she had exhibited as a Christian for all those years.

Overcoming Addiction

God showed Karen, however, that the controlling and dependent aspects of both relationships ultimately rendered them more a curse than a blessing. He also showed her how He, as her Bridegroom, was jealous of her affections. He conveyed His genuine desire to be Lord of that holy place within where she had given access to her lovers. And He compelled her to grieve over the state of her infidelity—the profound reality that she had bowed down before idols and had broken allegiance with her Husband, the One to whom she had committed herself for life.

Other Christians were central to this process. First, a handful of friends around her had become aware of her struggle. One in particular—Becky, who was mentioned earlier—had some insight into the struggle Karen faced in developing same-sex friendships. Becky had helped Karen out in the weeks following her separation from Susan. And as a result, Becky had the closest access to ongoing temptations Karen faced—in particular, the difficulties surrounding the second relationship.

However, Karen distanced herself from Becky at that time,

not wanting anyone to check the unqualified enthusiasm she was experiencing in the friendship. Becky knew this and simply prayed for Karen while giving her ample opportunity to connect with her. That access gave Karen options. She knew that another was there to help *when she was ready*. Becky had the good sense not to press too hard too soon, entrusting Karen to the Lord.

God came through. At the kinship group (a small home fellowship that was part of the church both Karen and Becky attended), someone received a word of knowledge concerning a person buckling under the weight of an illicit relationship. The word applied acutely to Karen. Unbeknownst to anyone, she and her friend had fallen sexually a few days before. Karen grabbed Becky after the group, confessed what had happened, and began to come out of the fog of her addictive and idolatrous pursuit of this friend.

But that was only the beginning. Karen also tended to withdraw from fellowship. Becky and a few others helped her by remaining steadfast sources of love, especially during the painful process of recognizing her sin and letting go of the relationship. The ache remained for Karen, and that aching aloneness needed to be covered. But Becky also knew that Karen could become inordinately dependent upon her, heightening expectations she could not meet. When she perceived that neediness on Karen's part, she would initiate prayer.

Through prayer, Becky helped to establish Jesus as Karen's primary nurturer. She didn't step in as Karen's mother substitute but instead planted images and words that mediated the maternal presence of Jesus into the deep void in Karen's soul. And He began to reveal new dimensions of His love to her. Not only was He her Husband, but He was also the deep, soothing presence that could touch and sustain her as her mother never did.

Now, instead of denying that need or submitting it to idols, Karen could seek Jesus. And in His presence, in that deep place in her soul where He had come to dwell, she learned to discern when other people were encroaching on the Lord's territory. His presence also freed her to begin to love others appropriately, without falling prey to making them into idols. With Jesus as the Lord and lover of her soul, she could walk out of addictive idolatry in peace, alive to new compassion and power.

The Sufficiency of Jesus

Karen came to grips with idolatry, Jim with narcissism. Both expressions of addiction had distorted their real needs for intimacy with God and others, and denial had played a big role in empowering their compulsions. But as the love of Jesus revealed the illusions and emptiness, both began to confess to others the struggles they faced in seeking love in whole and appropriate ways.

Gratefully, Karen and Jim had a handful of mature friends who mediated Christ's grace and truth to them. A great void of loneliness remained, but with the combined efforts of the indwelling Holy Spirit and the prayers and presence of loving others, that loneliness eased.

Jesus surprised each with His capacity to enter into the pain of old deprivations and wounds. He established Himself as the center out of which each could say yes to true intimacy and no to the broken, addictive imitations.

That rhythm of receiving real love and forsaking the false is essential for the addict. It takes time and requires a lot of confession and a lot of support. The addict's will to be free—and concrete steps taken in the right direction—must be encouraged and empowered.

Jesus is faithful, yet firm. He will not have us mastered

by false images and relationships. He wants us alive only to reality—the truth of His pervasive love and the hard, exhilarating and maturing path of learning how to love others without eroticizing them. Only He has the right to invade and master the deep heart out of which our longings for intimacy flow.

TEN

Freed to Love

While still a young Christian, as I grew in the conviction of God's capacity to free me from homosexuality, as well as His calling me to free others in His name, I moved into a new stage of refinement. Central to this refining was a change of schools; I transferred from my original college to UCLA. There I moved into a Christian fraternity house, which proved to be as much of a challenge as it was a blessing.

I was forced to come face-to-face with my fears and prejudices toward men—conservative, heterosexual men in particular. All my old ambivalence surfaced. These men represented tradition and orthodoxy, a kind of normalcy that

I felt inadequate to contend with, rejected by and, as a result, rebellious toward. Four of us shared a room, then moved and lived with another four the following quarter.

A great and unexpected realization broke through during my first year at the house. These men *loved me*. In spite of my unorthodox cultural trappings (long hair, sharp tongue, black humor), they called out the good in me and indeed blessed me. Sometimes they loved harshly. One man admonished me to repent of my prideful and elitist spirit (a defense against being rejected, but a sinful one). Yet for the most part, my brothers loved me by praying for me and encouraging me to grow in the Lord.

It surprised me to discover whole men who could love another man freely, even affectionately, without erotic intent. I remained a bit cautious at times. Still I bathed in the distinctly masculine affirmation I received from these men. When I felt safe enough to open up and be vulnerable to a buddy in the house, I experienced an unparalleled sense of wholeness. I was one of the guys, and I loved it. I realized I was finally enjoying true same-sex love as God had intended it to be.

Through that live-in experience, Jesus granted me courage. He enabled me to stand in His strength and to exercise the gifts He had given me. For the first time I received feedback that I possibly had preaching and counseling gifts.

I began to define myself as a dynamic agent of God's kingdom and not merely as a "recovering" homosexual. I enjoyed a real sense of worth rooted in His love and purpose. I felt incredibly alive to the greater picture of seeking the Lord first and reveling in His provision. That provision became clear and consistent during the two and a half years I lived there.

The experience confirmed one essential truth: when Jesus

reigns in strugglers' hearts, love is liberated. Not only are they freed to receive genuine, nonerotic love from others, but they can give it as well. Jesus reorients their relational base, which includes motivation, the storehouse of good gifts they have for others, and the reservoir of unmet needs for intimacy and identity. He enters into all those areas and begins a new and unified work.

In regard to motivation, Christian strugglers realize that discovering one special friend, or even several, is not an end in itself. The greater desire sparked by Jesus involves the advancement of God's kingdom on the earth. Alive to Christ's triumph over evil and the reality that many are still blinded to Him, strugglers join with other believers to mediate that triumph to each other and to a broken, unbelieving world. As in my life, strugglers discover personal strength and gifts that God begins to use. Quite unselfconsciously, they become alive to much more than their brokenness—they've become a part of God's solution to a broken church and a dying world. (We will explore this in greater detail in chapter 12.)

But personal needs for intimacy and identity remain. And for those legitimate needs to be met by others, Jesus must establish a new work within strugglers that liberates those needs from falsehood. The logic is simple. If my needs are still shrouded by old wounds and current addictions, I may be rendered *unable* to receive the good, straight-ahead offerings of my Christian friends.

Much of this has already been explored. We've seen how the breakdown of early relationships can dispose a person to projecting that breakdown onto others who evoke the memory of those early relationships. And we've seen that the healing of sexual brokenness requires the presence of Jesus as revealed in the depths of one's own soul and in fellowship. Both are crucial. To know Jesus, we need to be known by other Christians. And yet the life of Jesus within one's soul can sustain us as we walk the often difficult path of maturing into whole relationships within the body of Christ.

For example, Karen's need for the Spirit's presence was very different from Jim's. The Spirit helped her to practice His presence as the key to separating herself from two idolatrous relationships. Reattaching to healthy, supportive relationships was another task. She needed to learn new boundaries that would allow the expression of deep need without compelling her to forsake all boundaries and make an idol.

Jesus is helping Karen with this crucial boundary-setting as she allows Him to root Himself within. The journey isn't easy; it readily evokes the fear of needing too much, of becoming too dependent. But she now confesses to Him regularly her desires for intimacy, and she submits new relationships to Him. That grants Him the freedom to establish Himself as *the* boundary between Karen and her new friends.

Jim's boundaries, instead of being too thin, were too thick. Except for his addictions, he remained detached from others. The Holy Spirit jogged him into *the will* to fellowship. He genuinely didn't want to; he felt content in the control afforded him by isolation. But in obedience he began to fellowship. And through his interaction with others, the Lord surfaced in him the judgments and bitterness he held toward men, as well as Jim's fear of actually feeling needy for men.

As we've seen, Jesus has begun to heal these hurts and to empower Jim as he wills to engage in a healthy way with both men and women. Through His indwelling Holy Spirit, He enables him to walk through his fears into genuine friendship.

Both avenues of God's healing presence—binding up old wounds and making whole relationships in the present—must be kept open and explored thoroughly. The two frequently converge, although a different season of healing may be marked more by one avenue than the other. I frequently see imbalances in this area, however, and the result is a weakened sense of wholeness.

Some helpers, for example, insist on the pivotal role of healing in the restoration of the sexually broken. That healing more often than not occurs over a short, intensive period that is outside one's local church context. God may accomplish great inner healings during that time. But often the healed return home to a fellowship context that supplies *no real relational structure* on which their growth can be supported.

With no whole, intimate relationships, strugglers have no one with whom to live out the healing. Some churches often offer great fellowship opportunities but no avenues for the deep healing many need. As a result, strugglers may continue to feel utterly alone or utterly vulnerable to perverse possibilities.

A balance is clearly needed between the deep healing and sustaining presence of Jesus and the living out of that healing in Christ-centered relationships. The two together create a whole person.

Pressing Into the Christian Community

For strugglers to press into the community, they need to grasp two keys about the Christian community. The first is the just-disclosed truth that freedom from homosexuality must involve whole relationships with others. The second involves the posture and patience required to enter into healing relationships.

Christ's indwelling presence in no way frees people from needing others; it simply enables them to need others in a normal and appropriate way. Until Karen received more healing of her need for mother love, she was vulnerable to grasping erotically after women as maternal substitutes. Until Jim became more rooted in his own goodness as a man, he was tempted to seek personal completion through erotic encounters with men. But neither excess discounts Karen's need for maternal love or Jim's need for distinctly masculine care. And with Jesus as one's personal center and catalyst of a new community, strugglers can and must pursue these avenues of relational wholeness.

A personal illustration may clarify this. When the Lord revealed deep voids in my life for love and attachment, I sought and found Him. He began to reveal Himself as the Father who could touch me deeply in those dry and walled-off regions of my soul. But He didn't permit His care to be enough, just as He didn't create Adam to be reliant solely on Himself. Adam was graced with an inspired need for others, as was I. And I submitted that deep cry of my heart to my wife and a small group of trusted friends who met weekly for prayer. The Father continued to fill that void through their love and prayers as I conveyed my deprivation to them.

The void isn't full yet. But just as the apostle Paul instructed us to be filled with the Spirit again and again, so must I submit my emotional deprivation again and again to those I love and trust. I am "being filled." And the Lord has clearly revealed that He intends for that infilling to occur not only through His personal presence, but also through the love of people who uniquely provide for me that which I did not receive in my early relationships.

Concerning one's posture and patience in receiving this infilling, strugglers may be set up for disappointment when they find that most Christians are unwilling or unable to grant them that kind of deep care. Many of our brothers and sisters aren't very "therapeutic" or even understanding regarding sexual issues. That's why the posture of each struggler must be strengthened and tempered by Christ's presence. He sustains us as we *will* to grow in fellowship with others.

Paul, a good friend coming out of homosexuality and currently a Living Waters coordinator, describes it well. He realized early on that he could assume responsibility only for his own actions and reactions to others in the church; he couldn't base his commitment to the church solely on others' immediate commitment to him. He had the realistic expectation that it would take time to develop healing and intimate friendships. In the meantime, he could hold fast to Jesus as he became more knit into the body. At times his social and emotional needs were met; at other times they were ignored, even treated clumsily and without understanding. Jesus gave him grace to give to those who were graceless toward him. And Paul developed a handful of significant friendships within which he could share the deep affairs of his heart, including his sexual struggles. To insist on that level of intimacy right away would have been a boundary violation for Paul and others.

Judy, a faithful Desert Stream participant, experienced an incredible molding of honesty and the witness of her new "creatureship" in Christ at a small home fellowship group. She had fallen into sexual sin with an old lover. Surprised at her capacity for such behavior, as well as discouraged and ashamed, she slouched into the meeting. She had vowed not to confess her failure to the group. But as she worshipped Jesus and experienced His love and the love shared between the worshippers, she broke.

Still teary-eyed, Judy initiated the sharing time by confessing her fall. Some knew her vulnerabilities only in the abstract, so they were a little startled. All were sobered, for in Judy they glimpsed their own failures that had gone unconfessed.

The leader of the group initiated prayer, and all followed by laying hands on Judy as she sought to lay the burden of guilt and shame at the foot of the cross. All heartily agreed with the leader as he spoke Christ's word of forgiveness to her.

After the prayer, Judy received some of the most meaningful encouragement ever. One woman reminded her that she wasn't starting over; instead, she said, the deeper repentance and reliance on Jesus following the fall would create in Judy something even more precious to Him. One of the men thanked her for her honesty. He told her rather clumsily that because of her beauty in the Lord he had forgotten she came out of a lesbian background. Another sister encouraged Judy to call her during the week if the temptation seemed too rough to face alone.

Judy left that night a little shaky but deeply moved. Love had embraced her. In the depth of her confession Jesus entered through His people and administered grace and truth.

The Need for True Intimacy

But Judy, Paul and every struggler need more than a place to confess failure and receive encouragement; they need relationships that help secure their true identities as gender persons. Through ongoing, ever-deepening intimacy with others, they can receive the blessing that's essential to owning and becoming alive to one's maleness or femaleness.

Close relationships with both sexes are crucial here, but different. In the same way that the same-sex parent affirms a child's gender from a vantage point distinct from that of the opposite-sex parent, so do peer relationships convey to strugglers a different kind of gender affirmation and challenge, depending on the gender of the friends.

I underscore the need for *real intimacy* undergirded by trust. And trust has three components in my definition: commitment to one another, commitment to wholeness and commitment to the advancement of God's kingdom. Trust in the friends' goodwill and loyalty liberates a receptivity to the other's blessing; mistrust prompts detachment, as many experienced with parents. Trust awakens the weak aspects of one's gender to come into the light, to grow. Formerly walled-off areas of the heart become known; then they can be empowered to become a part of one's whole person.

I think of Jonathan, a good friend who called forth in me a flood of deep longing for bonding with the masculine. I had been detached from that need. And in the light of his trustworthiness and commitment, I could own that need and incorporate it into our friendship and the greater fabric of my manhood.

Similarly, while in the early days of my relationship with Annette, she elicited in me strong feelings of masculinity that compelled me to desire her, to long to protect and serve her. I wanted her—man to woman! Jesus' healing preceded that release, but Annette was the unique feminine vessel who called forth my heterosexual response.

For the struggler to trust another, both parties must also genuinely will to be whole. As a person admittedly weak in sexual self-control and gender identity, I must ascertain my own desire for freedom from homosexuality and that of my fallen friend. That means checking my tendency to eroticize the other.

I wouldn't have permitted my heart to open up to Jonathan had I not trusted my own commitment and his to wholeness. I'm simply too weak. I might not be able to distinguish healthy same-sex love from the erotic and idolatrous were it not for

171

the tried and true allegiance we both pledge to Jesus. Likewise with Annette. I wouldn't have responded to her heterosexually had she not demonstrated her own commitment to personal wholeness.

Trust is readily broken when that commitment is violated. One person's perception of the other's benevolence is shattered when the supposed commitment is found to be fueled primarily by erotic love. Similarly, manipulation and other veiled, conniving efforts to control the other's affections break trust. For friendships with either sex to effect gender wholeness, both parties must *will* personal wholeness and *forsake* broken, hidden agendas.

Finally, the trust that inspires healing intimacy always keeps in mind the greater goal—Jesus and His kingdom. Another person's love is never an end in itself. *Its goodness is always assessed by the degree to which it better enables both parties to grasp and live out Jesus' will for their lives.* The end is allegiance to Jesus. Intimate friendship informs one's greater purpose as an agent of intrinsic value to the body of Christ.

Trust in the greater reality of God's kingdom within the relationship also inspires trust in one another. We no longer feel utterly alone in attempting to find the love we have so desperately sought before. One greater prevails. That faith in God's presence and sustaining power is crucial, especially given a history of relational abuse.

Making Peace With Their Gender

With Jesus' help, strugglers must make peace with those of their own gender for several reasons. First, they need the affirming love of others in order to awaken the reality that they *are* adequate and normal gender persons. Such friendships can also provide healthy role models that help guide the strugglers' own journey toward gender wholeness.

Finally, intimacy and appropriate affection provide a much-needed balm for the years of same-sex deprivation and rejection.

But that intimacy stirs up the old homosexual yearnings. Strugglers will be sorely tempted to eroticize the other and control this newfound resource of healing. And those immature feelings must be allowed to come up and be deposited at the foot of the cross. Without facing and surmounting the fear of their remaining tendencies, strugglers are left either to fantasize or suppress those feelings and flee from legitimate sources of same-sex love.

God wills that we not be overcome by evil, but that we overcome evil with good (see Rom. 12:21). If strugglers are honest with God and with objective others, confess the feelings of infatuation as they arise and release them to Jesus, they make a profound discovery: that process of naming and forsaking clears the way for whole same-sex attachment to occur.

That need for same-sex bonding becomes de-eroticized as strugglers submit to the Lord the initial tendency to sexualize the other. And when the erotic temptation has passed, the need for same-sex attachment remains. The latter can be even more frightening in its power and intensity.

But strugglers must face their neediness. The children within—naked and grasping—extend their small hands to the lost fathers or mothers of youth. Will you love me? Will you be patient with me? Will you reject me? cry the children. They stand on the edge of a chasm that widened with each rejection of their own gender. In fear and trembling, they now seek the hand of those who can meet them at that point of need and help bridge the gap of alienation. In psychological language, that placement of unmet childhood need onto adult relationships is known as ''transference.'' The detachments from same-sex love sources of old now seek attachment in present, ongoing relationships. Finding those with whom strugglers can discover nonerotic intimacy is critical. Strugglers *must* make sufficient peace with their own gender. Failure to do so impedes their progress toward heterosexuality. To encounter the opposite sex effectively, they must first be resolved with their own gender. That means facing the need for same-sex attachment, discovering healing avenues of friendship and becoming more rooted in their adequacy as gender persons. (Special thanks to Elizabeth Moberly for her insights concerning the same-sex attachment.)

The key conflict for strugglers is the fact that other people do not exist as their lost father or mother. The need to transfer childish longings does not mean there are ready-made parents who can sustain the weight of that need. Obviously, broken, sexualized relationships were strugglers' first efforts at transference. These failed due to their eroticism and idolatry—the fact that the lovers had to carry the weight of all the other's need! They couldn't, nor can any whole relationship in the body of Christ.

It's a dilemma for strugglers, especially those whose backgrounds are unusually deprived of same-sex love. The human tendency is to seek to control the love object that appears trustworthy and accessible. But we have no right to control others, no matter how needy we are.

That's where the practice of God's presence is absolutely critical in the face of learning to befriend another. Strugglers need continually to yield up to the Lord the beloved friend, prayerfully recognizing that the other first and foremost exists in relation to the Creator and His will. No matter how broken or needy strugglers may be, they must yield their childish control that would seek to conform the brother or sister to a parental image they can never satisfy.

Only in yielding the need and the relationship to the Creator are strugglers truly freed to receive the good gifts their friends may want to offer them. Their perspective needs to agree with that of Bonhoeffer:

> God did not make this person as I would have made him. He did not give him to me as a brother for me to dominate and control, but in order that I might find above him the Creator. Now the other person, in the freedom with which he was created, becomes the occasion for joy....God does not will that I should fashion the other person according to the image that seems good to me, that is, in my own image; rather, in his very freedom from me God made this person in His image. I can never know beforehand how God's image should appear in others. That image always manifests a completely new and unique form that comes solely from God's free and sovereign creation.[1]

My own journey in identifying the deep need for same-sex love, then meeting that need in whole friendships, has been difficult but exhilarating. I had been ignorant of the need during the first few years of my Christian walk. It wasn't until the homoerotic addiction ceased that I felt a strong emotional pull for men. As a single person, that need started to be met in the Christian fraternity house and at church. After I was married and became steeped in domestic, ministry and seminary demands, I no longer had much time for same-sex friendships. So the need surfaced illegitimately in an addiction to pornography, and that red-flag warning compelled me into therapy and a good, hard look at the relationships that were key to bearing my unique needs and burdens.

I felt pretty raw about the whole matter. Several prospective friendships began to sour during my time in therapy. Either I or the other person was more committed to the friendship for various reasons, so intimacy and trust never deepened. One friendship became close, then quickly changed as the friend moved on to other interests and relationships.

The Father opened my eyes, however, to a couple of good friends with whom I had a long-standing history but whom I had never considered intimates. Quite unselfconsciously, I felt the Lord deepening my desire to invest in those relationships. One of these men was the aforementioned Jonathan, and the other's name was Mark. With both I experienced the trust and intimacy required to share deeply; with either I could be vulnerable and receive the deep affirmation and care for which my heart yearned.

Tapping into that need frightened me. I feared idolatry, was occasionally tempted to eroticize them, and often became depressed when I felt slighted by either of them. At times I wanted to forsake both friendships as a way of controlling my neediness. If I couldn't conform them to my expectations and demands, I thought, reverting to old habits, I could control my heart's uncertainty by walling them off altogether. Better to be detached than hurt.

But God had different plans. He wanted to temper that needy child, to grow him up so that he could stand within me. The Lord also helped me to accept what my friends could and couldn't give, making it clear that no relationship could ever meet my needs perfectly. What else would compel me to seek Him first as my daddy and my provider?

Finally, God made it utterly clear that these relationships were merely vessels—not only of the healing I needed, but also of the greater work of His kingdom. These two friendships had a higher purpose than merely how whole I became through them. They will be measured ultimately by the degree to which all parties involved are more conformed to Christ's image and will. (For more information on same-sex intimacy, please see the *Pursuing Sexual Wholeness* guidebook, chapter 18 and appendix articles 4 and 11.)

The Father has furthered His will for me through my male friends. I feel more alive to my masculinity as a result of them. The temptation to romanticize or eroticize the other is burned off by Him who reigns as the Lord of the friendship, compelling us to sharpen one another's vision and strength for the advancement of His kingdom.

Prior to an intensive ministry time, Jonathan and I were praying together. Side-by-side, not face-to-face, we sat, awaiting God's hand of anointing. In a profound way, Jonathan mediated the gracious presence of the Lord to me. The love I felt for him in that moment was but a glimpse of the awesome glory of God that encamped about us.

That interaction enabled me to carry out God's will powerfully in the days ahead. It also opened my eyes to what lies beyond our earthly status. I received a glimmer of oneness with the Lord, free of any fallen qualifications.

I rarely experience such moments. They can't be manufactured or controlled anymore than intimate, inspired relationships can be. But I praise God that He sees fit to use brothers and sisters to mediate such divine encounters. They heal the soul; they've helped secure mine. And through same-sex friendships, God has seen fit to further His kingdom. Amen!

Moving on to Heterosexuality

As we've seen, resolving who we are in relation to our gender must occur in order to press on into heterosexuality. And press on we must. Same-sex relationships, however whole and inspired, cannot be strugglers' relational end. They must face squarely the reality that God calls His children to discover who they are through relationship with the opposite sex. As we've seen, His image is revealed in the union of male and female.

The yearning to merge with the opposite sex will occur at different times and with different intensity for each struggler. Much depends on the degree of personal resolve with one's own gender. For example, as I grew more secure in my masculinity and in the whole relationships that affirmed it, I desired to break out of primary same-sex relationships and into heterosexual dating. I came up against the limitation of trying to find completion *in the same gender*.

Something mysterious and different called me in the form of a woman. I had dated long before any homosexual exploits. But this time, having recognized my brokenness as a man and having sought healing for it, I began to date as a whole, heterosexual person. Past experiences with women usually digressed into a kind of neutered buddy-buddy arrangement in which I was more tempted to identify with her rather than encounter her as the other. But through God's healing work in my gender identity, as well as my heeding God's call to be reconciled to the opposite sex, heterosexual desire burst forth in me.

I felt as if I were seeing women for the first time. Possessing a beauty, appeal and power all their own, they captivated me—and frightened me a bit, too. Could I carry out a relationship with her? Would she find me attractive? Would I be man enough to pursue her, even if it meant possible rejection? I felt as if adolescence had finally arrived in all its awkward, unbridled authority.

Gratefully, Jesus continued as the Lord of this sexual adolescent. And once again, in the same way His presence makes all the difference in whole same-sex relationships, so it does in the pursuit of opposite-sex ones as well.

My relationship with Annette is a testament to the faithfulness of Jesus. In my ignorance and innocence in heterosexual *savoir faire*, the only real initiative I could take with her was spiritual. All I could insist upon was the lordship of Jesus in our relationship. All I could ascertain was that both of us sought Him first for ourselves on behalf of our relationship. That gave Him the authority to work in both of us more of the essence of His image.

By that I refer primarily to the way Jesus helped round out our gender identities through the other. Jesus healed Annette and me not only prior to the relationship, but also through it. That understanding reveals the dynamic nature of whole heterosexual relating: one becomes more whole through the relationship itself.

As our relationship deepened, the Lord revealed to me how my prior homosexual unions were fueled by an intense, childish need. But now, with Annette, God was calling me to stand and love her as a whole person. He wanted me to give to her, to provide for and protect her, not to seek her childishly as a phantom parent or messiah. That posture of manly servitude would be my completion! And Annette needed my masculine care in order to shed the veil of false strength and self-protection that guarded her heart. For her to embrace more of the fullness of her own femininity, vulnerability and gentle responsiveness, she needed me to serve her.

The following illustration may clarify this. Early in our courtship, Annette called me in a state of despondency. I didn't know what the problem was, nor did her tense, desperate phone call convey much except her need for me. I honestly didn't want to see her. I was busy, and frankly I felt put upon. I wasn't even sure I loved her at that time.

Begrudgingly, I entered her apartment. There she sat, looking altogether orphaned, like someone still in shock following the loss of a loved one. She could barely speak. We didn't grasp until much later that Annette's periodic bouts of depression were due to ongoing emotional and spiritual oppression caused by sexual abuse. All I could do at that time was put my arms around her and hold her in all her unloveliness and unnamed brokenness. I held her until she wept. I felt God's strength empowering me as a man to love the woman He would call to be my wife. And in that safe and secure place, Annette allowed the real pain and need to surface. She softened in the strength of my presence.

That afternoon marked a change in our relationship. Shortly thereafter I experienced erotic feelings for Annette as never before. *I felt manly* in relation to her. Out of that masculinity, I yearned for deeper communion, a true and whole urge to encircle and become one with her. I knew then that I wanted Annette for my wife. Before God, I knew I was man enough to commit myself to her for life. (For more information on heterosexual relating, please see *Pursuing Sexual Wholeness* guidebook, chapter 19 and appendix 12).

Jim's journey into heterosexuality was marked by learning how to set appropriate boundaries with women. Like many male strugglers, he didn't have an aversion to women on a friendship level. It was only when the female friend became romantic toward him that he felt smothered and even sickened at the prospect of physical intimacy. Much of that related to his mother, who had violated his boundaries as a male throughout his life.

Consequently, assertive women who expressed romantic interest automatically connoted "mother." Jim felt reduced to a weak little boy who existed to appease mother's needs and anxieties. But he learned how to distinguish between his current female friendships and his mother. And as he established more healthy boundaries with his mother, he also developed the strength to pursue the women he desired and to set friendly boundaries with those whose need for intimacy he *didn't* want to meet.

Karen is taking small but significant steps in making peace with the opposite sex. She now recognizes the limitations of burying herself in intense same-sex relationships. Slowly she's learning to trust in the Lord for many of her intimacy needs while spreading out her need for human feminine care amongst several friends (as opposed to investing in ''one special friend'').

God has also begun to heal much of Karen's hatred and bitterness toward her father. As He does, Karen is opening up to the possibility that men may actually possess some important qualities. Trust grows slowly in her. But through healthy, nonthreatening friendships with Christian men in her church, Karen's misconceptions are breaking down. Her heart is softening.

A great help to Karen has been the committed friendship of a married couple. Their Christ-centered, honest approach to love and marriage has given Karen her first close-up look at a whole heterosexual relationship. They model wholeness, answer her questions and make her feel like a part of the family.

One evening while eating dinner with them, Karen received an unexpected healing. She observed the husband helping the wife bring out the food and serve the kids. In that brief moment Karen got a profound glimpse of the goodness of heterosexuality. God used the family to mediate His order and intention. He ministered His image to Karen's heart, and she was changed. No longer could she honestly retreat into the safety of lesbianism. Having received that picture of heterosexual wholeness, she resolved more than ever to realize that image in her own life.

God heals strugglers in order to free them to love others according to their true identities in Him. And He uses healthy relationships to reveal who strugglers really are. By His healing presence mediated through relationships, God reorders His fallen, needy creation.

But even unmet need has value—it compels strugglers into the sufficiency of Jesus and His Father. In the next chapter, we'll explore the incredible redemptive potential of unmet need, of wounds not yet healed.

ELEVEN

The Gift of Woundedness

At that point in my liberation from homosexuality when I could stare distinctly homosexual options in the face—gay lovers, an undergirding pro-gay theology—and choose the truth, I began to experience a new degree of freedom. This was the start of a vision for helping others come out of homosexuality. Earlier I had proclaimed my desire to do so but had been strongly exhorted to consider getting my own act together first. Sound advice. I couldn't very well help pull someone out of the fire when I was consistently getting burned myself. But now I was gaining momentum in my sexual resolve and stability.

While vacationing in Europe, the Lord confirmed to me

His desire to use me in freeing homosexuals. I was dancing in a London disco and felt increasingly oppressed. Not only was I being lured by the power of others' sexuality, but also by my self-absorption; I was strangely drawn to my own image reflected in the mirrored dance hall.

I left feeling bound by a restless yearning that I knew could never be satisfied. Once into the night, I began to call out to the Lord. Immediately He released me, and I received an incredible empowering of His Spirit that caused me to laugh and dance as I made my way through the Hyde Park district.

Then a man walked by, obviously gay, who turned back to seek me out as a sexual partner. Much to my surprise, I responded with the joy of the Lord. "I will not have sex with you," I replied, "but I would love to tell you about Jesus." He looked surprised but interested. We continued to walk, and I witnessed to him for about two hours. We stayed in contact throughout my stay in London. In no uncertain terms the Lord was commissioning me to minister to homosexual strugglers.

Later, around the time of Annette's and my engagement, the pastors at the Vineyard asked me to give my testimony before the church. I did, and its enthusiastic response prompted Kenn Gulliksen, the founder and head pastor, to encourage me to start a support group for people struggling with homosexuality. He had met many Christians in the Los Angeles area whose homosexuality prevented them from moving into the fullness of Jesus and His church. As a result, many stood on the sidelines, believing in Him but remaining in the gay community. So, with the church's blessing and Annette's support, Desert Stream was born out of a weekly support group-Bible study for gays seeking Christ in the heart of West Hollywood. Clearly this was a ministry

I could have, only because I knew the struggles and Jesus' sufficiency personally.

In a similar way, whereas sexual brokenness once threatened to destroy Jim and Karen, God transformed that vulnerability into His healing opportunity. Now, out of that weakness that God has chosen to indwell, Jim and Karen proclaim His faithfulness to others. He knows them intimately, and His grace and restorative power flow out of their depths. That flow continues outward to those in the church and the world who desperately need Jesus. As Joseph said to his brothers who sold him into slavery, "You intended to harm me, but God intended it for good to accomplish what is now being done, the saving of many lives" (Gen. 50:20).

Redeemed sexuality gives life; unyielded sexuality constrains it. Sexuality is critical to our personhood and spirituality. Far deeper and broader than mere genital contact, sexuality involves how we perceive ourselves as gender people and the kind of boundaries we establish in relationships with others. That's why broken sexuality can become such an avenue of spiritual darkness. When the yearning to know and be known becomes empowered by evil, sexuality jumps its track and careens chaotically outside of God's will. The devastation wrought by the sexual failures of key Christian leaders confirms the power of sexuality gone awry; it helps us to grasp the truth that *unsubmitted* sexual brokenness pollutes one's whole being and can pollute the church as well.

But the power of Jesus can become an inexhaustible source of cleansing and humility, a testament to God's faithfulness and sufficiency to resurrect lives dying under the weight of sexual and spiritual brokenness. Karen and Jim are experiencing that thorough indwelling of the resurrected One. As a result of submitting their brokenness to pastoral care, to friends in their local church, and to others within the Living Waters program, they're seeing Him make inroads into all aspects of their lives. Each is learning a new center out of which to love people of both sexes, new boundaries with which to love appropriately, and a new sense of who each truly is as male and female. Both are dealing with the past hurts and relationships that helped shape their sexual brokenness. They're also facing and learning to forsake the addictive patterns that now arise with less frequency.

Both Karen's and Jim's sexuality is indeed an instrument of God's awesome healing grace. His ministry of sexual redemption is transforming their humanity and giving them a fruitful ministry.

The Rhythm of the Cross

This healing work issues out of the rhythm of the cross. Neither Jim nor Karen can afford to live anywhere but under its shadow. Their healing depends on His presence; the Holy Spirit continually calls each to identify with Christ's death and be empowered by His risen life. That rhythm is at once humbling and mighty, and its mightiness bursts into their lives at unexpected moments.

Sometimes in worship, Jim feels a oneness with Jesus that transcends all fallenness, all the qualifications of his earthbound state. He touches on the boundless potential of that divine encounter—Christ in him, the hope of glory! But the moment passes, and he leaves the worship service. Driving home, the cares of the world encroach upon him, and he feels tempted to search out men who arouse him, who embody some strange blend of confidence and macho eroticism.

But instead of falling into sin, Jim submits himself to the reality of Jesus' bearing the weight of all brokenness, sin and immaturity. He humbles himself before the crucified One.

He agrees once more with the sufficiency of Jesus to uphold him in his fallen state. Christ's grace proves sufficient once more, and he makes it home safely.

The cross constantly reminds both Jim and Karen that Christ's kingdom has broken into this world. He has assumed the brokenness of their homosexuality and resurrected Himself in their humanity. But the cross also points to that hope of the kingdom yet to come, the time of Jesus' return, when we will no longer bear about in our earthly bodies the groanings of this fallen world. Then we'll know the boundlessness of being face-to-face with Jesus, worshipping Him in unqualified freedom, in a state light years away from any concerns about sexuality, gender or boundaries.

The cross reminds us that we live between two kingdoms, the one revealed through Christ's first coming and the culmination that will occur upon His return.[1] The cross further enables homosexual strugglers to live peacefully within that interim period, delighting in the healing work being wrought by the resurrected One within the depths of their sexuality.

God's Purposes

Like all sinners, homosexual strugglers must realize that Jesus is the goal. He is our mark, our Redeemer, our sustaining presence. As we walk closer with Him and toward His will, we become whole. And that wholeness won't be completely realized until we see Him face-to-face in glory.

Two keys can be drawn from this realization. First, since Jesus is the goal, personal wholeness is *not*. Our priorities must be ordered correctly. When strugglers make perfect heterosexual responsiveness the mark, they subordinate Christ's call to discipleship to a static psychological ideal. They become increasingly whole as they will to follow Him;

sexual reorientation occurs out of spiritual conversion. A much greater calling lies before us all than mere hetero-sexuality.

Second, we cannot expect to experience a complete absence of sexual struggles in this lifetime. Our sexuality is basic to our humanity, which continues to bear the marks of this fallen age. That means the homosexual struggler may still experi-ence homosexual temptations; the abuse victim may at times feel irrationally threatened in certain situations; the former sexual addict may need ongoing accountability in his area of weakness. None of that minimizes God's healing power. It simply places that healing in the dynamic process of *becoming* whole, a process that will never end until we see Jesus in heaven. (Please see *Pursuing Sexual Wholeness* guidebook, chapter 14.)

What the struggler can reasonably expect is to become *whole enough* in this lifetime to sustain fulfilling, heterosexual relationships. By that I mean the capacity to relate intimately but nonerotically with the same sex, and the freedom to encounter the opposite sex as a desired counterpart—with interest, not fear or distaste. Jesus desires to grant us that capacity because He realizes how essential it is to revealing God's image, as we saw earlier.

Personally speaking, that means God wills and enables me to develop whole same-sex friendships. I may be erotically tempted in them, but that temptation lessens as I grow more whole. Jesus has freed me from sinning in such relationships. Furthermore, Jesus has granted me enough heterosexual desire and personal maturity to love a woman, take her as my wife, and oversee a household and growing family. I do so through the healing of my uniquely masculine soul that secures me as a *whole-enough* husband and father. His grace upholds me throughout every domestic twist and turn. Flurries of homosexual feeling cannot shake the rock on which I stand—Christ Jesus.

In this lifetime Jesus does not intend to satisfy every craving of the soul, to remove every weakness. For our deep longings are for Him above all else. That longing within us is not merely the result of personal brokenness or the influence of family and friends; it's intrinsic to our status as the created, as children disposed to grow upward to the Creator, through His love. Our fallenness highlights the folly of attempting to secure ourselves on the earth, through the creature. The Father employs the aches and longings that remain to keep us focused on Himself.

But His purposes don't end there. He desires to employ that which has yet to be healed as an avenue of His grace. Through the wounds and deprivations that He indwells, God creates in us a deep wellspring of compassion—His heart— toward others who are broken. He graces us and intends to use us to grace others.

Annie Herring, singer and songwriter in the musical group the Second Chapter of Acts, expresses well how God employs our wounds as instruments of grace. In her song "Love Comes and It Goes," she writes of a human heart pleading for love and yet broken, unable to contain love like a cracked jar that can't hold water. Jesus enters the heart and heals it. For the first time, love as expressed in His grace finds a resting place. But the cracks remain.

The song ends as it began. Love that has entered the heart will go, only this time for the purpose of offering to others the grace received. Jesus has entered and revealed His healing grace in the brokenness of the heart. And as Annie describes, we allow the wounded, cracked places to become the wellspring out of which flows His powerful and altogether personal gift of grace to others.

While giving a series of lectures on sexual redemption one time, I felt consumed with a longing for distinctly masculine love and affirmation. I ached for it. I felt frustrated that my male friendships could not wholly meet that need, and more frustrating still were the broken patterns I could still observe in my relationships with them. I felt tempted to entertain lustful masculine images. And I resented God for all of it—the neediness that remained in me, the strains of neurotic dependency, the temptations. Most of all, I resented His intangibility in the midst of my struggle.

While walking to my lecture on ''healing'' (laugh track, please), I finally broke. I cried out to the Lord, and He responded simply: ''I have been tempted in all ways as you've been, yet without sin. I know your struggle. My grace is sufficient for you.'' I wept as He poured out His mercy into my dry and cracked heart. I wept even more as I considered those attending the lecture I was about to teach and how their hearts needed that same mercy and grace. God equipped me that morning to minister His grace with an authority and authenticity I had never experienced, and that grace proved healing to others.

Becoming a Wounded Healer

Two keys about becoming a wounded healer (a term coined from Henri Nouwen's excellent book *The Wounded Healer*) involve authority and authenticity. First, what gives one the authority to heal others in light of one's weakness? Doesn't the latter disqualify one from service? Certain unsubmitted weaknesses, especially those that digress into sin, *can* render one's service destructive. Consider Karen, who prior to submitting her lesbian struggle for healing fell with a woman to whom she was ministering.

True healing implies that we're aware of our weaknesses

190

and that those weaknesses are submitted to Jesus and others who can help us deal with them effectively. That prevents our weaknesses from polluting our service to others. The best thing I can do for a friend or client to whom I'm sexually attracted is to confess that reality to someone other than the desired person. That enables me to establish healthy boundaries with the person and to be held accountable to those boundaries. Then I'm free! My authority to heal remains intact. Those weaknesses are then liberated to become sources of strength.

God's power meets me at the point of confessed impotence. He reveals His heart; He shows me again that my weaknesses and woundings are the ground in which grows His deepest work. There I've been humbled, and there Jesus continues to reveal His resurrection authority and grace. Poured out again and again on my weaknesses, that grace fuels my authority to heal. He has proved His sufficiency and strength, and that grants me all I need in order to extend grace powerfully to others who are broken.

That also frees me to be wholly authentic with others about my "unhealedness." I have nothing invested in covering my difficulties. To do so would only obscure the powerful witness of His sufficiency! Any narcissistic need I have to hide behind an image of unqualified wholeness ends up binding me. It bars others from offering me grace and light where I need it most. I need the freedom to confess my weaknesses to others in order not to be constrained by them!

Wounded healers must forsake the prideful tendency to be defined only in terms of strengths and wholeness. *They must will authenticity*, especially where they're still weak and tempted. That liberates the witness of God's incredible sufficiency and makes real that sufficiency through others who mediate Christ's grace and truth.

But does that healing extend only to those who come out of homosexual backgrounds? Gratefully, no! The struggler begins to recognize in his quest for intimacy and identity the struggle familiar to all.

Symptoms may vary. Some face heterosexual brokenness, others the sterile temptation to isolation. Whatever the specifics, the struggle to emerge as a whole person upheld by whole relationships applies to every man and woman. The struggler must grasp that fact. And the profound healing that Jesus has wrought in the struggler's life applies to all. As Leanne Payne states, ''The healing of the homosexual is the healing of all men.''

The insights and healing interventions detailed in this book have emerged out of a decade of my ministry, primarily to homosexual strugglers. But the principles and redemptive experiences described here clearly extend far beyond the realm of homosexuality. No one is exempt from sexual brokenness—no one is altogether whole in his capacity to love and be loved. Therefore, no one is exempt from the ever-deepening work of healing that Jesus wants to establish in the sexuality of His people.

God intends to use the wholeness He has wrought in homosexual strugglers to bring wholeness to many. Commissioned as wounded healers, these men and women will spark a healing revival within the church, as we shall see in the next chapter.

TWELVE

Becoming
Part of the Solution

Desert Stream Ministries thrives today only because of its rooting in the church that birthed it—the Vineyard Christian Fellowship. I, the struggler, need the church! My freedom depends on my connection with fellow believers. Beyond any therapist, any parachurch support group or any isolated healing experiences, I need the greater expression of Jesus revealed in the local church. Recognizing this in my own healing helped determine Desert Stream's insistence from the beginning on remaining within the church.

Like all Christians, strugglers grow into wholeness through commitment to the full range of earthen vessels found within each local congregation. As they identify with the bigger picture, they identify less with the problem at hand. Their emphasis on the "symptom" of homosexuality broadens with the recognition of each Christian's struggle for intimacy and identity. Christ's faithfulness to strugglers broadens to include His faithfulness to all people regardless of the precise nature of their struggles. Only in ongoing, awkward and inspired interaction in a local church can the strugglers shed a morose overemphasis on the problem and become part of the solution.

Karen, for example, in the midst of her healing process, grew depressed as she considered the depth of her need and how vulnerable she remained to idolatrous relationships. She was tempted to isolate in that season. Through the encouragement of some close friends, she didn't but continued to attend faithfully her kinship group.

As Karen's vision broadened to include a handful of heterosexual women, she realized how pervasive the theme of idolatry was in *their* lives. They were bent toward men, either obsessed with them or depressed without them. Karen saw in their struggle a glimpse of her own, only they weren't calling it what it was—idolatry. Meekly, Karen raised the parallel to one of the women and pointed out how Jesus needed to heal her through His lordship and through nonbinding relationships.

The women received her exhortation. And through that interaction, God released Karen from the fear of her own brokenness, her peculiar perversion. He freed her to discover her fallenness in the greater body of Christ—and to interject His solution into the body as well. (For more information on how crucial the role of the body of Christ is to the struggler, see *Pursuing Sexual Wholeness* guidebook, chapter 17 and articles 9 and 10 in the appendix.)

The Desert Stream Program

Those who seek freedom from homosexuality within Desert Stream Ministries find two things. First, many profound issues in their lives need to be identified and submitted to Jesus for healing, as this book clearly shows. Second, that healing must be walked out within the local church. God's plan for each struggler includes becoming a dynamic part of God's solution to a broken, faithless world—Christ's body, the church.

Let me explain further how we facilitate this two-fold plan. Our main offering is an intensive healing and discipleship format entitled Living Waters. The essential components of that program are contained in the guidebook to which I've referred throughout this one. Basically, strugglers walk one week at a time through the ever-deepening process of identifying the pain and brokenness associated with their sexual struggle, while simultaneously discovering the awesome sufficiency of Jesus and His people in those areas.

The climate is loving, the subject matter intense and matched only by the powerful presence of Jesus in the midst of the group. Strugglers become *known* there—no more masks, no more hidden sins, no more defensive reframing of a problem that's destroying them. And Jesus reveals Himself as we worship, as charismatic gifts are stirred up and help guide the healing work at hand, as the teaching proceeds, and as individuals forbear one another in confession and prayer. Jesus establishes His lordship, His love, His order in the depth of each participant's sexuality.

About half of these people are involved in our local church; the rest come from churches throughout Southern California. A few move into the area simply to attend the Living Waters group. At any one time, Desert Stream may sponsor four or five Living Waters groups that operate not only in our church, but also in other Los Angeles-area churches. And we also provide an annual training seminar for church leaders who want to be equipped to implement these groups in their own context. At this time, approximately twenty such groups are being sponsored by churches around the world.

Throughout the program, we urge participants to make good their commitment to their own churches, or to choose a church and commit to it. The program concludes on the note that each struggler can and must move beyond problem-centeredness. That occurs naturally as one discovers his gifting and purpose within the body of Christ. (For more information on this, please see *Pursuing Sexual Wholeness* guidebook, chapter 20.)

Making a Contribution

Homosexual strugglers who have truly submitted them-selves to the healing process can make a tremendous con-tribution to the body of Christ. In fact, they're sorely needed to strengthen and round out the church. "Graduates" of Living Waters receive much healing and many insights about the healing process that are relevant to the majority of their fellow church members.

I see reflections of this consistently. The healing that strug-glers have received ignites a deeper honesty and faith within the church. Members of kinship groups who hear the con-fession of a struggler's vulnerability are less fearful of con-fessing their "normal" heterosexual brokenness. At the same time, the victories over sin and disorder—be they conveyed by verbal praise reports or dramatically through the marriage of a former homosexual within the church—spark the hope of Jesus' capacity and commitment to restore willing hearts, regardless of the type of brokenness.

Furthermore, the intensive kind of discipleship exemplified

by a Living Waters group and required of strugglers who sincerely want to be free lays the groundwork for church leadership. An unusually high percentage of lay leaders within the Vineyard of Santa Monica are graduates of Living Waters. They bring to their ministry an unusual degree of integrity and reliance on the power of the Holy Spirit.

What accounts for this rare blend of character strength and anointing? Once again, the healing of the homosexual struggler reveals some key insights that can contribute powerfully to the building up of the body of Christ.

The first insight involves a recognition of one's powerlessness and, as a result, an utter reliance on Jesus. There's not much middle ground for strugglers seeking freedom. They can't stay too long in self-deception, in those soulish "gray zones" where many grow comfortable and eventually atrophy.

Strugglers wise up quickly to the intense reality of spiritual warfare. In that battle they're either covered by Jesus or vulnerable to the enemy. They recognize that the powerful and shifting field on which the battle is being waged is their sexuality. Without His light and protection, Satan can lance their sexual vulnerabilities and pierce the heart. With the help of others, the strugglers recognize that forsaking Jesus' lordship for lesser gods means a return to bondage.

Honest and Yielding

That reliance on Him becomes tempered and deepened by two things: ongoing honesty with others and a continual yielding to God's supernatural, healing presence. Both of these factors either make or break one's success in the Living Waters program.

By their very presence, all strugglers own up to certain weaknesses, blind spots that necessitate the light of others' vision and prayer. Coming to the gut conclusion that only Jesus can make the difference leaves little room for delusions of grandeur. God honors humble hearts. He enters in and deepens His healing work in those who are genuinely sick and tired of their own lies and illusions. Repentant strugglers know this.

They likewise learn how to listen to the Creator's voice in this dynamic process of becoming. They begin to pray accordingly for self and others, receiving from them that deep, prayerful mediation of God's intention.

Homosexual strugglers who seek freedom thus exemplify honesty about personal weakness and an openness to God's renewal. They become true supernaturalists. The order and wholeness of their lives depend on One greater who lives in them.

Strugglers also come to see that intimate relationships with other Christians are critical to healing. And recognizing the tendency to flee relationships or to race headlong into them, they learn to let Jesus provide the balance and a new set of boundaries that make all the difference as they seek to work out their salvation through fellowship with others.

In short, homosexual strugglers who have truly submitted to the healing process become known—by God and by others. They no longer hide in fear, in the shroud of silent, shameful struggle. Light breaks into the darkness. At the core of their being, a seat that includes sexuality, Jesus is enthroned. The process of healing remains painful and at times is belabored. But Christ reigns to reorient the struggler. Having been given access, He identifies that which needs healing and provides the grace and power needed to effect that healing.

Such a personal, powerful move of Jesus sparks allegiance. The struggler wants to serve the soul's healer and Lord. No abstractions here—Jesus has entered in and reclaimed a life written off as dead. In the most intimate place and manner imaginable, He demonstrates His sovereign love. For the healed struggler, no real option exists but to lay down one's life for Him who saved it.

The aforementioned qualities—reliance on Jesus in the face of powerlessness and a raging spiritual battle, honesty and accountability in areas of confessed weakness, faith in supernatural healing, loving others through Christ's love, and living out of that dynamic center where Christ dwells, free from shame and hiddenness—all these mark the lives of strugglers I know within my church who have submitted themselves to healing. God has appointed them as key leaders in the church. He has entrusted them with tending to and raising up men and women to carry out the work of His kingdom.

At a recent meeting of church leadership, Jim, our head pastor, asked for testimonies about the dynamic presence of God in ministries throughout the church. Five of the seven who spoke were former Desert Stream participants. All proclaimed how God moved mightily in their midst, revealing Himself through signs and wonders in various meetings. Suddenly I realized that God was indeed anointing these leaders with an increasing amount of His powerful compassion.

God has thereby used the potential tragedy of homosexual struggle to plant the seeds for revival. He plans on employing each yielded vessel significantly to build up His body and draw all people to Himself.

The Ministry of Desert Stream Graduates

Let me describe some of these Desert Stream graduates to you and the vital role they play in the life of the Vineyard Christian Fellowship of Santa Monica. Karen continues to deepen her commitment to the church. She is content learning how to receive from God and others, rather than busily pursuing ministry.

Jim is especially keen on intercession. He also remains committed to evangelism and to operating more fully in the gifts of the Holy Spirit.

Tim functions prophetically, particularly in regard to the sexual immorality that besets our church and the surrounding culture.

Craig's gifting in healing prayer expresses itself in helping out with the church's prayer ministry. He also helps educate the church on how to pray effectively for others.

A victim of sexual abuse herself, Ruth volunteers in the C.R.O.W.N. Club, the Vineyard and Desert Stream's offering for children with abuse backgrounds.

Jonathan began and now oversees a large teaching and service ministry to persons with AIDS. He trains and equips members of our church and churches throughout Southern California for such ministry. He also leads support-healing groups for Christians with the disease.

Bev just had a baby; she and her husband await clear direction about their desire to be missionaries.

Brad, now married, functions as a legal advisor for the church. He also oversees and teaches Desert Stream's oldest support group for men.

Michael leads one of the church's kinship groups. Because of its success, he is intent on raising up new leaders to plant a new kinship group.

Jody works as the assistant director of Desert Stream. As a former missionary, she is pursuing deeper involvement in the church and in ministry.

Like every struggler who has truly yielded to the healing process, Jody needs the church very much. There the specifics of her struggle are swallowed up by the brokenness of all people and, gratefully, Christ's commitment to redeem that brokenness. But God has something greater in mind for Jody, Karen, Jim and all strugglers in the process of becoming whole. He intends to use them to spark revival, to help prepare Christ's bride for His return.

The church needs the struggler! Out of the profound work of restoration that Jesus has wrought in each life will flow healing authority. Jesus dwells there, full of grace and truth. But He's not content to stay. He insists on bursting out of each struggler to proclaim His faithfulness in resurrecting the dead. He will heal wounds incurred by homosexuality; He will be glorified in the honest testimony of His healing authority. Through the struggler's restoration and resulting ministry, the church and the world will be awakened to His powerful love.

Notes

Chapter 1

1. Dietrich Bonhoeffer, *Life Together* (New York: Harper & Row, 1954), p. 20.

Chapter 2

1. Karl Barth, *A Doctrine of Creation*, vol. 3 (Edinburgh: T and T Clark, 1936), p. 290.

Chapter 4

1. Bonhoeffer, *Life Together,* p. 116.

Chapter 7

1. Alan P. Bell, Martin S. Weinberg and William Hammersmith, *Sexual Preference* (Bloomington: Indiana University Press, 1981).

Chapter 8

1. George Rekers, *Shaping Your Child's Sexual Identity* (Grand Rapids: Baker, 1982), p. 139.

2. Elizabeth R. Moberly, *Homosexuality: A New Christian Ethic* (Greenwood: Attic Press, 1983), pp. 1-10.

Chapter 9

1. Patrick Carnes, *Out of the Shadows* (Minneapolis: Comp Care, 1983), p. 19.

Chapter 10

1. Bonhoeffer, *Life Together,* p. 93.

Chapter 11

1. George Eldon Ladd, thesis of *A Theology of the New Testament* (Grand Rapids: Eerdmans, 1974).

Bibliography

Anderson, Ray S. *On Being Human*. Grand Rapids: Eerdmans, 1982. An excellent theological study of what it means for humanity to be created in the image of God and to seek out that meaning through the church.

Athanasius. "On the Incarnation of the Word." *The Nicene and Post-Nicene Fathers*, vol. 4 (second series). Originally written: 318 AD. An ancient essay that probes the depths of what it means for Jesus to assume our broken humanity and so free us from the confines of sin and death.

Atkinson, David. *Homosexuals in the Christian Fellowship*. Grand Rapids: Eerdmans, 1979. A thorough, evangelical perspective on the clinical and theological angles of homosexuality.

Barnhouse, Ruth Tiffany. *Homosexuality: A Sexual Confusion*. New York: Seabury Press, 1979. A thoughtful look at how morality in the late twentieth century is being determined more by science than by sound theology.

Barth, Karl. *The Doctrine of Creation*, vol. 3. Edinburgh: T and T Clark, 1936. Exhaustive theological work that probes the utter significance of God's creating man in His image as male and female.

Bell, Alan P., Martin S. Weinberg and William Hammersmith. *Sexual Preference*. Bloomington: Indiana University Press, 1981. Landmark survey of the backgrounds, attitudes and behavior of male and female homosexuals.

Calvin, John. *Institutes of the Christian Religion*. Grand Rapids: Associated Publishers. Originally written: 1559. Comprehensive work which remains the foundation of reformed theology.

Carnes, Patrick. *Out of the Shadows*. Minneapolis: Comp Care, 1983.

The best book available on understanding sexual addiction.

Cook, Colin. *Homosexuality: An Open Door?* Boise: Pacific Press Publishing Assoc., 1985. A concise, readable examination of the relevance of Romans 6-8 to the homosexual struggle and victory.

Durham, Charles. *Temptation*. Downers Grove, Ill.: InterVarsity Press, 1982. A sensible, solid handbook for battling the three kingpins of sexual temptation—the world, the flesh and the devil.

Foster, Richard. *Celebration of Discipline*. New York: Harper & Row, 1978. A brilliant introduction to spiritual disciplines and their relevance to Christians today.

Guernsey, Dennis. *Thoroughly Married*. Waco: Word, 1975. An insightful, Christ-centered approach to the nuances and gut-level realities of making a marriage work.

Hurst, Ed. *Laying the Axe to the Roots*. St. Paul: Outpost Ministries, 1980. A profound look at the various sins that undergird homosexuality.

Inrig, Gary. *Quality Friendship*. Chicago: Moody Press, 1981. An excellent look at Christian friendships that is as biblical as it is practical.

Ladd, George Eldon. *A Theology of the New Testament*. Grand Rapids: Eerdmans, 1974. A brilliant biblical theology that centers on God's kingdom having come to us in Christ and the culmination of that kingdom when Christ returns.

Lewis, C.S. *The Weight of Glory*. Grand Rapids: Eerdmans, 1965. Another awesome work by one of the greatest Christian writers of the twentieth century.

Lowen, Alexander. *Narcissism: The Denial of the True Self*. New York: Macmillan, 1983. A provocative, psychological study of narcissism. Relevant to homosexual strugglers, although clinical in nature and not written from a Christian vantage-point.

Lutzer, Erwin. *How to Say No to a Stubborn Habit*. Wheaton: Victor, 1984. A sound, Christ-centered guide to overcoming problem behaviors.

Missildine, W. Hugh. *Your Inner Child of the Past*. New York: Simon and Schuster, 1963. A helpful accessible study of how our experiences as children affect us as adults.

Moberly, Elizabeth. *Homosexuality: A New Christian Ethic*. Greenwood: Attic Press, 1983. A groundbreaking reevaluation of the psychodynamic roots of homosexuality. Dr. Moberly emphasizes the homosexual's deprivation of same-sex love needs and his striving to repair that deficit through homosexual relationships.

Bibliography

Moberly, Elizabeth. *Psychogenesis: The Early Development of Gender Identity*. Boston: Routledge and Kegan Paul Limited, 1983. A far more clinical version of *Homosexuality: A New Christian Ethic*, without specifically Christian references.

Nelson, James. *Embodiment: An Approach to Sexuality and Christian Theology*. Minneapolis: Augsburg, 1978. A bold and creative look at theology and sexuality that succeeds in some points and fails miserably in others; for example, the chapter on homosexuality.

Payne, Leanne. *The Broken Image: Restoring Personal Wholeness Through Healing Prayer*. Westchester: Crossway, 1981. An excellent, beautifully written book that for the first time exposes the roots of homosexuality to the healing presence of the Holy Spirit.

Payne, Leanne. *Crisis in Masculinity*. Westchester: Crossway, 1985. Another great work that extends the healing presence beyond homosexuality in order to include other "symptoms" of sexual and emotional brokenness in men.

Peck, M. Scott. *The Road Less Traveled*. New York: Simon and Schuster, 1978. Written in Peck's pre-Christian days, this book manages nonetheless to detail the key themes that make for human wholeness and maturity.

Rekers, George. *Shaping Your Child's Sexual Identity*. Grand Rapids: Baker, 1982. In spite of an occasional reactionary edge, Rekers expertly draws from his vast clinical experience in order to explain the need for a child to become secure in his gender identity.

Ross, Michael. *The Married Homosexual Man: A Psychological Study*. Boston: Routledge and Kegan Paul, 1983. A survey of the attitudes and patterns of married men with homosexual tendencies. Its tone is highly clinical and nonreligious in nature.

Sqroi, Suzanne. *Handbook of Clinical Intervention in Child Sexual Abuse*. Lexington: D.C. Heath and Company, 1984. A comprehensive clinical guide to sexual abuse. Very helpful, although nonreligious in nature.

Smail, Thomas. *The Forgotten Father*. Grand Rapids: Eerdmans, 1980. A sensitive, profound examination of how our Christian theology and experience must be rooted in the primacy of our heavenly Father.

Thorkelson-Rentzel, Lori. *Emotional Dependency: A Threat to Close Friendships*. San Rafael: Exodus, 1984. A must-read booklet for any homosexual struggler seeking intimate same-sex friendships.

Vanauken, Sheldon. *A Severe Mercy*. New York: Bantam, 1977. An autobiographical account of the loss of a spouse. At points it illuminates the meaning of loss; at others, it breaks under the weight of the author's flowery prose and implicit narcissistic tendencies.

White, John. *Eros Defiled*. Downers Grove: InterVarsity Press, 1977. One of the first solid evangelical approaches to sexuality. Excellent on most issues, but fails to provide hope for the homosexual's reorientation; instead, White advocates behavior change apart from real inner renewal.

Wilson, Earl. *Sexual Sanity*. Downers Grove: InterVarsity Press, 1984. A clear biblical guide to dealing realistically and uprightly with one's sexuality in an idolatrous age.

If you need help or know
someone who does, please contact:

Desert Stream Ministries

P. O. Box 17635

Anaheim, CA 92817-7635

(714) 779-6899

Fax: (714) 701-1880

E-mail: info@desertstream.org

Website: www.desertstream.org

If you enjoyed *Pursuing Sexual Wholeness,* here are some other titles from Charisma House that we think will minister to you . . .

Old Man New Man   ISBN: 0-88419-741-7
Stephen Strang   Retail Price: $13.99

Respected journalist and publisher of *New Man* magazine, Stephen Strang addresses the deeply personal habits that can make or break a man. In this book filled with godly insights and practical suggestions, men will find real answers from God's Word about marital tensions, financial stress, sexual purity, getting in shape, impacting their children positively and much more.

Imprint: Siloam Press
Breaking the Grip of Dangerous Emotions   Janet Maccaro, Ph.D., C.N.C.
ISBN: 0-88419-749-2   Retail Price: $19.99

Learn how to stop letting dangerous emotions rob you of your joy as you discover the truth about worry and stress. You can replenish your physical body with a cutting-edge nutritional program that will restore your health. Explore exciting and proven protocols for rebuilding and regenerating your body, mind and spirit.

Imprint: Siloam Press
Better Sex for You   Helen Pensanti, M.D.
ISBN: 0-88419-687-9   Retail Price: $14.99

Improve this vital area of marriage in a way that honors God. Dr. Pensanti offers suggestions and answers to some of the most commonly asked questions by using a frank and unique approach based upon medical knowledge, experience, godly insight and the Word of God.

To pick up a copy of any of these titles,
contact your local Christian bookstore or order online at
www.charismawarehouse.com.